How It All Began

The Life Of Derek L. Draper

Dedication

I dedicate this book not only to those who receive a copy at this time of our 60th wedding anniversary year, but to all future family members who will have the opportunity to read it at some future date.

As with all things in life, what I have written is as how I remember it. Others who have been parts of my life's journey to this point, may have experienced and seen it differently.

PAGE OF CONTENTS

Chapter 1 How It All Started.
Chapter 2 My Home
Chapter 3 Early Life
Chapter 4 Growing Up
Chapter 5 Coastal Life.
Chapter 6 Schooling & Sports
Chapter 7 Love of My Life
Chapter 8 At The Wheel
Chapter 9 Wedding Commitment
Chapter 10 Life is Good
Chapter 11 Canada Here We Come
Chapter 12 Planting Roots
Chapter 13 Our Spiritual Change
Chapter 14 Never a Dull Moment
Chapter 15 First Country House Built
Chapter 16 Christmas in The Outback
Chapter 17 Back to The City
Chapter 18 Caring For Others
Chapter 19 To See The Sea
Chapter 20 Run For My Life
Chapter 21 Dear to My Heart
Chapter 22 Kelowna Break
Chapter 23 Sail Away?
Chapter 24 Next Phase
Chapter 25 Mexico Diary
Chapter 26 Thoughts of England
Chapter 27 Back Across The Ocean
Chapter 28 Home Again
Chapter 29 Service To Others
Chapter 30 Renovation Desire Returns
Chapter 31 Refilling The Retirement Vessel
Chapter 32 Step Back To Travel
Chapter 33 Moving Forward
Chapter 34 Present Time.
Chapter 35 Thoughts About Life

Chapter 1 | How It All Started

As I sit here in Kelowna in the year of 2023, having lived through a pandemic, and being of sound mind (which I know not how long will last), I wish to let my family know that I have had a wonderful life and am grateful for all the children, grandchildren and great grandchildren that have become part of this life.

As you read my story it covers much, but with all life's journey's I have had ups and downs. In this book I will only point out the ups because the downs have helped me get to the ups.

* * *

I was born into this world on October 29th 1942 in Willesley Castle Derbyshire, UK, home of the Earl of Derbyshire.

Willesley Castle

I was born so far away from London (where my parents lived at the time) due to World War 2 raging in England. London was especially dangerous and the government felt that expectant mother's should leave London prior to given birth. They went north and stayed there until after the birth of the child.

My mother stayed in a home in the village nearby, but I have no information regarding it.

Willesley castle, home of the Earl of Derbyshire, had been converted into a maternity hospital by the Salvation Army for the duration of the war. Today there is a plaque on the outside wall stating that over 4000 children were born there during that period.

The Plaque at Willesley Castle

Chapter 2 | My Home

*Our family home at **229 Ladysmith Road Enfield Middlesex,** was the only house I lived in before I got married. It was a two story-building semidetached with a garage. There was only a short period during the war when a bomb damaged our house that we had to relocate while it was being repaired. Other than that brief relocation, this was my only childhood home.*

My birth home: 229 Ladysmith Road, Enfield Middlesex.

My grandparents on my mothers side lived next door to us, which meant I had a very close relationship with them. My grandmother was blind so she relied on my mother and the four boys for assistance.

Left: Older brother Geoff. Right: Baby Derek.

I still remember the wire going across our driveway, 10 feet off the ground, stretching about 15 feet long. It went from one kitchen to the other, with a bell attached to it so my grandmother could ring us for assistance when required.

I never met my father's parents.

When my father (Albert) was just 10 years old, his mom died and his father remarried. The new wife didn't want to care for all the children and kicked Albert, along with his sisters and brothers, out. He was 18 at the time and moved to London. Two of his younger sisters, Ella and Audrey, were adopted in Durham west Stanley and remained there all their lives.

I have never met either of them.

Chapter 3 | Early Life

Much of my memory from those early years of life relates to seeing the aftermath of the war. This includes bombed out buildings, ration books (which regulated the amount of food you were allowed to purchase based on family size), and taking the local bus to the places farther afield.

During the war sirens went off to warn us of an enemy attack. When these sirens sounded (which was usually at night), we had to sleep in a metal shelter in our back garden. Sometimes we'd go under a metal cover in our living room until the all clear siren came.

My father was exempt from going to war because of the work he was involved in. Instead, he was part of the home guard. Their responsibility was to make sure that when the nighttime curfew hit, there was a complete blackout with no lights that could be seen. Can you imagine walking about outside, completely dark, with only the moon to guide you? Imagine when there wasn't a moon.

My father also had an allotment (garden plot), about 600 meters from our house. It was in the fields I passed by it on my way to school. Throughout the war (and after too), he grew all the vegetables we needed plus more for others. Meat was expensive following the war, so we raised chickens and rabbits at the bottom of our garden. We never saw the killing but knew it had happened when you opened the pantry door to see either a chicken or rabbit hanging upside down with its head in a bag...or lack of a head if it was a chicken. Horses and cart delivered milk and bread just like you have seen in the movies. Shopping was a daily activity as we had only a small refrigerator. Following the war there was a great celebration and our community had a huge party for all the children in the neighbourhood.

I also had an elder brother, Geoff, who was two years older than me. It wasn't until I was about 12 or 13 years old that I discovered he was my step-brother. His biological mom had died in childbirth and my father had married my mom, Lily, when he was still a toddler. Neither of us knew anything different so I never suspected it.

Chapter 4 | Growing Up

When I was 5 years old I started school.

School picture of Derek

I went to George Spicer Elementary, and for the next 6 year I walked through the fields behind our house to go to school everyday. On the weekends the fields were turned into soccer pitches where everyone played. School uniforms were mandatory during my entire school life. I would say that this created an equal appearance for all. No discussion as to what to wear each day. It also denoted the school you went to - if problems arose outside of school, you were easily identified. In those days, your mom would take you to school for the first week, but after that, you were on your own.

My only claim to fame, was having my picture in the paper playing a triangle in the school band. Why was I playing the triangle? Because I couldn't hold a note with anything else.

George Spicer School Band | Derek in back row.

School provided lunch, which you paid a nominal amount.

Math, science and geography were the only subjects I managed to have a full grasp of. English was always a problem (and still is). Verbs, adverbs, nouns, and pronouns. Could never grasp the idea behind using them. I spoke how I felt, not if it was grammatically correct.

During these childhood years, we spent time by the southeast coast, Jaywick Sands. My parents, grandparents and relatives all had houses (bungalows) down there. Growing up in the 40s and 50s with family around was wonderful. It was great to have my grandparents (Arthur James Guest & Emma Clayton) live next door on **227 Ladysmith Road, Enfield.**

My great-grandfather on my moms side - Hezekiah Guest and his wife, Caroline - lived at **5-Ladbrooke Grove, Bush Hill Park.** This was only about 20 minutes from our home, and was in the same neighbourhood as even more family members (91 Alberta Road, Bush Hill Park). After church on Sundays my dad and I would go visit our great-grandfather, Hezekiah. He had a very pleasant manor. He was retired and always wore a bowler hat. He was also in good health and took walks around the neighbourhood. Quite the gentleman. I never met his wife, Caroline Ettridge, because she died before I was old enough to know her.

Walking was the usual mode of transportation, although our family did use the bus and train as well. Getting to the seaside at Jaywick sands, we would use a coach going directly to Clacton-on-sea, then a bus to Jaywick. And of course, we were always carrying two or three suitcases.

My family and extended family all went to church (although at different locations). I went to Sunday School most Sundays and sometimes had to push my little brother in a pram (stroller). Church was about 30 minutes away. By going to Sunday school, it did instil in me what was right and wrong, and to respect people - no matter how they acted or looked.

Television came to our house when I was 12 years old. Prior to that we went next door to Mr. Simmons. They had no children, so I assume they enjoyed having us come over.

As a side note about Mr. Simmons who I remember vividly. His toast had to be burnt and then the burnt part scraped off. This ritual was done each morning by his wife outside the kitchen door.

We listened to the radio for our news and sports update. Do you know what a radio is?

Looking back, I cannot remember ever having snow. It got cold but it just rained a lot, so it wasn't until coming to Canada that I knew what a snow shovel was.

I'm getting ahead of myself.

Chapter 5 | Coastal Life

Dereks Grandmothers Bungalow: *31 Glebe way Jaywick Sands*

The ocean has always been a drawing card for me. When I was either 10 or 11, my grandparents moved to Jaywick Sands (where we owned bungalows) which meant I would spend all summer down there.

My grandfather was a great beachcomber, spending early mornings walking the beaches and sifting the sand. He was looking for money fallen from the pockets of the beach revellers or anything that had washed up on the beach the night before. Nowadays you see people with metal detectors, but in those days, it was just pushing a fish net along the sand.

One day following a heavy rainstorm my grandfather went down to see if there was any salvageable items that had washed up on shore. He could not believe his eyes! There, drifting offshore, was a pleasure motor boat. He pulled the boat to shore, staked it to the shoreline, then made a salvage claim for the boat. It had broken loose above 4 miles up the coast.

While continuing his morning stroll he came upon a wooden clog, which he later found out belonged to a sailor that had fallen overboard in the English channel during the storm. He gave it to me, which I still have in my living room at this present moment.

The infamous clog

It was while I stayed on the coast with my grandparents that I gained an interest in construction. I helped my grandfather (who was a carpenter) do repairs to properties and I loved it. I'm not sure how much help I was.

One vivid memory I had was after the North Sea flood of 1953 on the east coast. I visited the aftermath and saw our bungalow, along with our relatives bungalows, had floated off their foundations.

My grandparents house was higher up, so although if suffered water damage it did not move.

That summer during my usual visit, I observed my grandfather and others moving their houses, as each had to be moved back to its original foundation. It was quite the project.

To this day the homes are still there.

Following the tragedy of the 1953 North Sea Flood (where 58 lives were lost), my father purchased a bungalow next to my grandparents, and sold the other property.

Another beautiful memory I have of my grandparents in Jaywick Sands relates to my grandmother sitting on her outside porch knitting. She recognized each person passing just by their voice, and carrying on a conversation with them.

It was while spending time with her I came to appreciate what it must be like to be blind, still having a fulfilling life. She made wool carpets, hall mats, sweater and most knitting project.

She lost her sight about 1934 and it was assumed to have been caused though the work she did. She was a French polisher, and the fumes affected her eyes. At this time my mother worked as a seamstress for the queen's dress designer Norman Hartnell but left to take care of her mother as well as her dad and two brothers, Dennis and Arthur.

Sorry to say but at present Jaywick Sands has determinated to become one of the least desirable places to live.

Chapter 6 | Schooling And Sports

During this period of time in my young life I became interested in soccer. We had about 16 soccer fields just behind our house - which on a Saturday were all being used. Although I played for my school, I never progressed any further. However, Geoff, my elder brother, played for the Enfield Town Youth Team.

I enjoyed going to see the Tottenham Hotspur play (also going by the name of SPURS) playing at N7 (try to figure out what location that means). In those days you only paid about one shilling, and it was standing only.

The school system in England is structured differently than in Canada. In those days, upon reaching 12 years you went to what you would call 'high school.' I went to Chase Boy's School. As you will see from the name it was an all-boys school...so no girl distractions.

Chase Boys School | Derek on third row, far left.

During this time, I took an interest in cycling and purchased a bicycle. How did I pay for it? Well, at the top of our road was a grocery store to which the people on the street would buy groceries. It being a long street, the elderly people would leave the groceries at the store and I would deliver them to their homes after school. I used this weird bicycle with a box on the front to deliver the food. It used to take about three trips.

In the mornings, seven days a week, I also delivered 50 newspapers that each had the address on it. London printed about 10 different papers each day. And then on Saturday mornings I helped the baker deliver bread to which I received 25 pence (plus a cake). So that's… how I paid for my bicycle.

One year our family went on holiday to Torquoy, in Devon. I decided to cycle there. It took me two days and I stayed in a Youth Hostel overnight (very popular in Europe). When I was about 14 or 15 I then toured Wales for three weeks on my bike and again stayed in youth hostels.

Back to school.

I enjoyed science, math and chemistry - which I now realize formed part of my interest in engineering. In my last year of school, I applied for an all-expenses-paid engineering apprenticeship with the government and had to sit through an examination.

*I arrived at the government building for the aptitude test and to my surprise, when I opened the door, there were about 100 or more other applicants. I nearly turned around and went home, but instinct told me to sit the test. Someone had to be one of the 9 people chosen for the position. Well, I ended up being one of the nine - so the moral is **never underestimate your abilities**.*

I had to sign papers - together with my parents - that I would complete the full five years. This entailed going to college two and a half days a week while balancing the time in the factory learning about the machinery and how to use it.

As a by-line to the above, I had also applied for a position in the air force and been accepted. But this would have required me to sign a contract for 12 years.

How life would have been different…

Chapter 7 | *The Love Of My Life*

The year was now 1959, and sometime in August, after having played soccer that afternoon, I went to a dance at the Southgate Royal. There, I asked this beautiful young lady for a dance. I remember her being the same height as myself (which has changed growing old), very slim and hair that was very professionally done up. I later learnt that that was her profession and I should expect the style to change weekly. I escorted her home via a bus (I did not have a car), and found out she lived only about 4 miles from me. I walked those 4 miles home afterwards. We were about 16 and 18 at the time.

Derek and Jennifer I When Engaged

As a footnote to our first meeting…

I got a phone call from Jennifer King (that being her maiden name), the following day asking me if I would like to come with her parents to the coast for the day. How she got my telephone number, as I am sure I never gave it to her, I still don't know.

This turned out to be a very scary outing. Her dad, who, up to one week beforehand, had only ridden a motorcycle with a sidecar had just purchased a car. In those days, you did not have to have a separate license or exam to drive. From the moment he picked me up, it should have been mandatory for him to take a test. That day I was going to learn how close you could drive behind a vehicle without actually hitting it. From my perspective siting in the rear seat of the car, that was the right place to be. I am sure the vehicle in front was only two feet away from his hood.

From that point on I preferred to take the bus.

As you might've guessed, the beautiful girl I met at the dance became my wife, the love of my life. Because I was only just turning 18, my future wife-to-be turning 16 years old, and having three more years of engineering to do, there was just no way we could get married. So we agreed we would only meet once or twice during the week and on Saturday's to go dancing. Dancing was usually at Wood Green Jazz clubs because we realized that we had similar tastes in music - traditional jazz.

Because the engineering apprenticeship position paid very little, they gave me free lunch. To earn some extra money, I joined the royal marine reserves. They paid me with the requirement to train one evening a week and two weeks training over the summer.

Derek in his Royal Marine Outfit.

Chapter 8 | *Life At The Wheel*

Having turned 18 years old now, I was the legal driving age to drive a car in England. My parent's purchased a car for themselves - a Morris 1000 - and then sent me to driving school to pass my test. After my second test I passed, and I then had to help my mum and dad to learn how to drive. My dad failed his first attempt and said he would never drive again - a promise he did keep - except he became a perfect back seat driver. Mum finally passed just prior to Jenny and I getting married (together with help from the local policeman training her and medication to calm her nerves).

I should tell you about my first car.

A friend contacted me offering a 1948 Hillman car. It didn't run, but with a little work to the engine it was put right. Unbeknown to my parents, I towed it to our house using their car and started working on it. Six months later it started. Well…I say started. It always needed a bit of 'encouragement.' Such as a little oil in the engine cylinders. When it started, the burnt oil in the engine cylinder came out as a cloud of smoke and you could not see for 50 feet behind me. I then sold it, being able to use my parents Morris 1000 car provided I kept gas in the tank and cleaned it.

To help give my mother practice, I'd go with her on her errands (when I was able), so she'd gain more experience without my dad. Cheaper, and more reliable for me.

Chapter 9 | Wedding Commitments

It was in my 19th year that we decided to officially get engaged, even though I still had 2 more years before my apprenticeship completion. By this time, I knew the timing was right, even with another two years before we would be getting married.

A friend of a friend sold rings at wholesale prices, and I remember him coming to Grandma Kings (Jenny's Mom) house with a wide selection to choose from. It was then that I learnt my future wife had very expensive taste. No more needs to be said.

Our wedding date was set for November 9th at St. Stephens church. The exact time I am not sure.

In England, prior to getting married, you have to apply to get a marriage license as well as a wedding announcement in the church parish you lived in. This took place three consecutive Sundays prior to the wedding. The Banns of marriage ('proclamations' as they were called), was to raise any canonical or civil concerns why someone should not be married. i.e. still married to someone else, etc. Being in a different parish's, mine was read out in St. Andrew's while Jenny's was announced in St. Stephens - where we were going to be married.

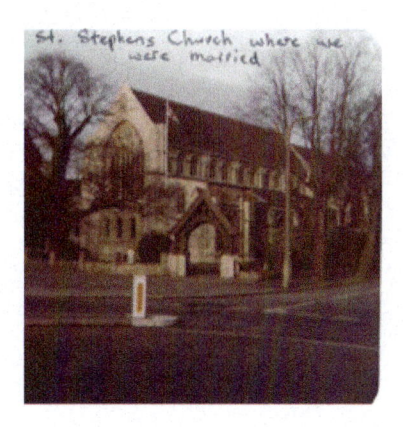

St. Stephens Church in Enfield England. The chapel where the Drapers were married.

Derek & Jennifer | Wedding Day, Nov 9th 1963.

Derek & Jennifer I Wedding Day, Nov 9th 1963.

The reception was then held at the parish hall at St. Marks Church in Bush Hill Park. One item that was interesting in arranging the reception was the wine. My family did not drink, whereas Jenny's family drank…not excessively…but they did like a drink. So, the compromise was they would pay for the wine and we would split the remaining reception costs.

Following the reception Jenny and I drove to Virginia Waters in the southeast of England and stayed in a hotel. Not sure if you are aware, but at English weddings it's custom for confetti to be thrown over the couple while departing from the church. While at the hotel, Jenny had to go to the washroom (which wasn't in our room), and as you can guess, out came the confetti all over the bathroom floor. Can you imagine her on her hands and knees picking up all the small pieces?

The next morning we were seated in the window for breakfast. Unbeknown to us, this was the seat they placed newlyweds at. So guess what? All the guests of the hotel were staring at us.

We only stayed one night at the hotel and then came back to our little flat. When I say little, I mean little. It was the ground floor of a converted large house. One living room / bedroom combined, a kitchen 6 x 4 feet with a sink and the smallest stove. We shared the bathroom with a couple next door. Our bed was the sofa during the day.

We absolutely loved it.

The first home of Derek & Jennifer Draper | Wellington Road, Bush Hill Place.

How did we get about? Well, we were known as 'the mods,' so we had a scooter. A little Lamdretta 100cc, which worked fine for the two of us. Except when it rained - which in England is quite often. Then it would stall. After about two months I managed to figure out the problem and resolved the stopping issue.

Chapter 10 | Life Is Good

Life was good to us. We lived on my salary and the money Jenny had earned since becoming engaged was saved. Within six months, Jenny had the money to place a down payment on a new house in Benfleet.

175-Seamore Ave. Benfleet.

Having purchased our first very own house, we moved in June 27th 1964. It may have been a new house but in those days the 'new house' had just bare wood planks as flooring, a kitchen sink unit, a pantry, one single bathroom and no appliances. We had to buy carpets and more furniture. The garden was unfinished, and Jenny got her first dog on January 8th 1965

Then came a time for a change. But first, let's go back a bit.

A position became available working in London selling commercial refrigeration units to stores and warehouses. It was November 30th, 1964. This position came with a car - which was good as I had a 40-minute drive to London each day - but it also gave us freedom to go out whenever we wanted to and not be limited by the weather (which the scooter did).

It was during this time, while working in London, that I went to Canada House on May 25th 1965 and inquired about immigrating to Canada.

Because of my engineering background work was available for me in Hamilton, Ontario, but Jenny had two cousins already in Calgary Alberta - Valeria and Pat.

So…we decide to immigrate to Calgary.

I mentioned to Jenny that it would only be for two years. She was very concerned about not seeing her family again.

We then had to tell our parents. So, June 8th 1965, having just been accepted by Canadian immigration, and a job lined up with an engineering company in Calgary, we told Jenny's parents (Wallace Bernard King and Gertrude Ivy Tickner King). It was June 14th and we were at the funeral reception of Jenny's grandmother - Eleanor Mabel Wallis King.

Not the best time to tell family.

Chapter 11 | Canada Here We Come

Placing our house on the market on May 31st and having been accepted for immigration, we left England August 13th, 1965

We flew to Calgary via Toronto, arriving in this cow town of about 250,000 people with just two suitcases.

Remember…we had left London with over 2 million people in the greater London area alone.

Derek & Jenny at the airport to fly to Canada

Although Jenny had cousins in Calgary, we were on our own. Within the first week, we had an apartment rented - 415-1333-13th Avenue SW - and furniture purchased (even though our money from England had not arrived in our bank account). Our personal items that were shipped in a wooden crate had also not arrived.

This was our first introduction to a credit card. In England you had no credit card. Pay cash...you know, the paper money.

On August 23rd I started working and realized after only the first month, that the apartment was too far from my work and we liked to be closer to downtown. We moved October 12th and got to know more people.

Life was good.

Even though I have a drivers license from England I still had to take a Canadian drivers test. Even though the driving was on the opposite side of the road as to England, it was an easier test as most cars - including the one we had - was automatic. I passed my driving test September 2nd.

It was around 1975 - approximately 10 years since leaving England - that we felt Canada would be our home for the future. By this time we'd been blessed with two children, Andrew and Tanya, so we applied for Canadian citizenship.

In those days you had to have a little knowledge of the country - which proved enough for it to be granted.

Derek & Jenny's Canadian Immigration

Jump forward fifty-four year…do you recognizes us? Me being only 5'4" bold and wrinkled with eight great-grandchildren. Jenny still as beautiful as ever.

Now back to the story.

Calgary was beginning to have a construction surge because of the oil industry, so I managed to get a position on January 7th 1966 with an architecture and mechanical engineering consulting company. I was a heating / ventilation designer which I felt had more future than the position I had arranged prior to leaving England.

Then to our great delight at the beginning of 1966, Jenny found out she was expecting a baby, which after two miscarriages in England, we felt having any children may not be for us.

It was also good timing as on April 20th, 1966 Jenny passed her driving test. This was not easy, because the baby bump in front of her was starting to get close to the steering wheel.

On September 22nd 1966 at 8.40 am, our first child, Andrew Lee Draper came into the world at 10lbs 8oz. In those days, fathers were not allowed in the hospital delivery room, so I had to wait patiently until Jenny was in the ward to find out if it was a boy or girl.

Although I was earning a good salary and had a nice two-bedroom apartment at #7-1834-14th street SW Calgary; upon news of Jenny expecting to, we needed many baby items. So two evenings a week (plus Saturdays) I drove a taxi as it allowed us to buy those needs. Not wants. Diapers in those days were made of cloth and not disposable, so they had to be washed. Not the nicest item to wash by hand so a diaper cleaning service was arranged. They picked up soiled diapers and delivered clean ones weekly. A great investment.

Our neighbours in the same building, Gene and Marie Kulsky, had a newborn baby within months of Andrew. Jenny did not have to work, so Marie and Jenny spent time together having 'baby talks.'

In May 1967 we moved again to 6205-4th street N.W - our third move in two years. We moved to an apartment owned by Jenny's cousins husband, Fred Walker, and we managed the building for him.

On July 7th - August 8th 1967, Jenny's parents came to visit giving them a chance to see Andrew who had just started to walk in June.

It was during the latter end of 1967 that Jenny realized she was expecting again. On July 29th 1968, Tanya Marie Draper came into the world, at 10lbs 2 oz - much to the delight of our little family.

Chapter 12 | Planting Roots

Now that we had two children who were both Canadian citizens, we realized that Canada was going to be our permanent country of residence and decided to buy a house. So we moved again to 7135-8th. N.W. We called it a 'soapbox on the hill.' It was brand new, very small and only $17,000.00 but served our needs.

When we decided to buy, we had no savings but acted on faith. Off to the bank we went and asked them for $1000.00, as this was the downpayment required. Then the bank manager asked us "How much are you putting as a downpayment on the house?" I answered, "The $1000.00 you're going to give us…" Surprised, he gave us the money and the mortgage, with payments of $125.00 a month for a fixed term of 25 years. All was approved and we became proud owners of a house. This started our days of renovating homes. This one had an unfinished basement, so that's where we started.

Life was very good to us in 1969; Jenny started selling Avon in April, which gave her the opportunity to meet our neighbours in the new area. Tanya took her first steps in June, and Christmas we went to England. It was our first time back since leaving.

It was interesting going back. Quite an eye opener, as we hadn't realized the changes in what was going to be our adopted country. Stores and houses in London all seem small compared with what we had in Calgary.

We stayed firstly with Jenny's parents.

While in England and it being winter, keeping the house warm took some doing. Most houses did not have any central heating, and relied solely on electric heaters in the bedroom and fireplaces in the downstairs living rooms.

One night after Andrew and Tanya had been tucked up in bed, we heard Tanya crying. Upon going to her room, we noticed that her lips were a blue colour, and she was so cold. We needed to turn up the heat.

Back to Canada.

Although I enjoyed working for the consulting firm, being in an office was too confining for me - even though I did inspections relating to projects we had designed.

So, when an offer in early 1970 to be a senior estimator for a mechanical contracting company came my way, I took the offer. This gave me the opportunity to enhance my career in construction.

You might ask how I could be an estimator from only working as a mechanical designer. That's because my position required that I estimate the costs of the projects which gave me the experience needed.

Not many months later in 1970, my work required that I relocate to Lethbridge from Calgary for about a 1 1/2 years as a Project Manager, starting our path of investigating the church.

Not knowing anybody in Lethbridge, we rented a house in a neighbourhood close to where I was going to work. Our neighbours were a couple of a similar age and had children about the same ages as ours.

Const. H. D. Doerksen and Ruth Steele
married Dec. 18, 1965

Harold & Ruth Doerksen

All was going well except they mentioned some interesting activities they do. I.e., Relief Society and Primary. Jenny became close with Ruth. Unfortunately, *before we had time to get to know them more, they moved to Calgary.*

Eventually, in September of 1971, we moved back to Calgary for the start of the new school year and unknown to us our old Lethbridge neighbours, Ruth and Harold Doerksens had bought a house just around the corner from the house we had left vacant when going to Lethbridge.

Chapter 13 | Our Spiritual Change

The friendship continued between Ruth and Jenny, and as our question about their church arose, they mentioned that there were missionaries that could help us further understand the gospel. So Jenny started having discussions, relating to the Church of Jesus Christ of Latter-day Saints.

At the same time, the project I was working on in Lethbridge still wasn't completed, so I was still commuting back and forth to Lethbridge, so they decided to wait until I was home.

Upon my return to Calgary, I started to sit in on the discussions, although not with a lot of enthusiasm.

My world was fine. I had a great family, good job, and attended a church that satisfied my needs at the time. Word of Wisdom was the only item I had to overcome. I did not smoke but did have a few drinks. My hobby however, was my beer and wine distillery in the basement of our house

Well, it all changed so I had to change too.

The basement distillery had to go, so down the drain it went. And the rest you know.

We were baptized on Feb. 1972, and in March 17th 1973 we were sealed in the Cardston, Alberta temple as a family for time and all eternity.

Realizing that Andrew and Tanya would be the only biological children we would be able to have, we made the decision to foster children with the anticipation of adoption.

In 1973 saw a lovely little ginger-headed boy come into our family. Jason, who was about 4 years old at the time and having been born in Edmonton Alberta on May 8th 1969 arrived.

Jenny and I had no idea that we would be able to adopt him, but as time went by the realization this may happen became apparent, and in 1977 (when he was eight), we were able to adopt Jason. He was sealed to us for time and all eternity on September 29th, 1977 in the Cardston Alberta Temple.

Chapter 14 | Never A Dull Moment

Although moving has been part of our lives - together with renovations - our next move was in 1973 and a little different. We moved to the countryside of Bragg Creek, which was 30 minutes west of Calgary. It was a log cabin, completely finished and on approximately an acre of land with no need for renovation.

What instigated the move?

Prior to the move, we had the house in Calgary plus this tiny cabin on Pine lake north of Calgary. It was just two bedrooms, but the second bedroom had two sets of bunk beds.

Pine Lake Cabin

Andrew, Tanya and Jason spent most of their time fishing off the dock at the cabin, or out in our neighbours boat fishing.

The only drawback was having to be at church on Sunday, which meant only Friday and Saturdays at the lake.

Having enjoyed the cabin and county life (even if only for weekends) we decided to sell the Calgary home on Huntervalley Road as well as the Pine Lake cabin and move to Bragg Creek in October 1973.

Bragg Creek was an exciting move.

Water came into the house via a well and sewage went into a septic field. We had power, a telephone and internet access too. The children would go down the road to a farm with a wagon to pick up our large containers of fresh milk.

On January 7th 1974, my parents - having been here for Christmas - went home just as the weather was getting colder and water into the house starting to freeze up

With plenty of land around us (there was an empty lot next door), the children had space to enjoy the freedom and explore. Reality came in the first winter in 1974. Snow, snow and more snow, to the point that on April 26$^{th.}$ (having survived the winter so far), we had a very heavy snowstorm.

It snowed so much that the power and telephone went out on a Friday. It was fun for the weekend, even though I went to Calgary to rent a generator so we could at least watch TV and run some heaters. By Tuesday of that week the novelty of no power had worn off and with the school still shut down, keeping warm meant sitting close to our log fireplace or a heater. We prayed for the power to return which I think it did by Wednesday.

It was during this time that we were attending the church on the northeast side of Calgary - where we had originally joined the church and resided from 1972. We got a call from the North Calgary Stake President who advised us that because Bragg Creek was on the south side of the highway into Calgary we should be attending the 4th ward on 17th Ave. SW. We had never given any thought as to the ward we should be attending but did as was requested.

Just prior to moving wards, Andrew (8), was baptized on October 5th after turning 8 in September.mFrom this ward we became friends with the Gedalman family, which I will write about latter.

On October 23rd 1974 while I was at work, I had a call from Jenny, stating that she had hit a pothole in the road and had left the road going into a ditch and laid the car on its side against the farmers fence. My first reaction was "Are you alright?" To which her reply was "Yes," but we weren't too sure about the car. I left work in haste and found Jenny standing on the side of the road and all I could see was the underside of the car. I am thankful to Heavenly Father that the farmers fence was there, otherwise the car would have been on its roof.

Chapter 15 | First Country House Build

When the winter had past and summer was approaching, we heard that the acreage next door was coming up for sale.

This was a whole new experience for us. We had renovated homes but had not built anything from the ground up. So in 1975 we drove right in and decided to build a country home. It was to be a cedar house (not made of logs) but pre-cut from large cedar planks.

Prior to starting the build we had decided to go to England for a holiday. Jenny left on June 16th with myself following July 15th and we both returned on July 28th. This meant that after the foundations had been poured, construction would stop until we all returned from England.

It should be noted that because I was working full time in Calgary and I could not afford to take too much time off, we decided to contract out most of the work on our build. But being me, I still needed to be on site to resolve any issues and inspect the work for compliance to code. That's why we paused the work while we were in the UK.

Having no services to the property meant we also had to arrange for someone to install the power, a telephone cable, a septic system and find water. The first three were easy tasks but finding water proved to be a lot harder.

We had a water diviner come out with his tools - which was basically just two pieces of wire. He held one piece in each hand and when he crossed over where the water lay below, the wires would react. You just had to hope and the depth was always unknown.

After he located water we employed a company to drill. They drilled 60 feet…no water. 90 feet…no water. 130 feet…some water but not a steady flow. It would have to do, as by this time we had overspent our water drilling budget, with the only drawback being the location - right under our front deck.

What was interesting was that our house we were moving from (next door) had water only 20 feet down.

Realizing that water year-round was going to be a problem, we dug a hole and buried a 3500-gallon water storage tank in the ground. This allowed us to pump water when it was available into the tank and drawing from the tank when it wasn't. Although the tank was in ground, the top was only 2 feet below the surface crating another problem.

Freezing.

To resolve this concern, we did what the farmers do with a horse trough and floated a heating pad on the top of the water inside the tank. Not enough to heat the water but enough to stop it from freezing.

By this time the house had been built and was ready to move in with no running water.

Not wanting to delay moving day, we decided to haul water from Bragg Creek for a few days until the storage tank and equipment was finally installed and ready to pump water.

Left: Our new home. Right: Our first Bragg Creek Property.

When the water finally started flowing into the house, you can just imagine the relief we all felt. You try carrying 5-gallon containers 100 yards from the creek.

It was nice water though.

Chapter 16 | Christmas In The Outback

Christmas time 1975 arrived at Bragg Creek, so we decided to get the biggest Christmas tree we could find. Our property backed on to the First Nations land and having made friends with some of them, (we had a 500-gallon gas tank on the property, so we gave them some when asked), we were given the right to select any tree that had fallen / or had been cut down on their land.

So off we went as a family in search of the perfect tree…and we came back with a tree that we felt was the right height. Our living room being in the centre of the house was two stories high, about 18 feet. It wasn't until we'd carried the tree back some distance that we discovered it was 22 feet, and very wide at the bottom. It was never going to fit in the room. So out came the saw and off with a few feet top and side. The other problem was decorating it, but that was resolved with the use of a high ladder. The result was wonderful.

Having no school in Bragg Creek required Andrew, Tanya and Jason be bused to school in Spring Bank. Each day the bus came by to pick them up. One day as they were returning home from school a wheel came off the bus, which was a surprise to Andrew. It's not everyday you see a wheel jump up at you from outside the bus. Fortunately, there were two wheels on that side so no danger. Another day Andrew was not seated and hit his head on the overhead rack when the bus hit a pothole. He cut his head but no brain damage.

The community was quite small, but there was a desire to have a kindergarten classroom. So, the old schoolhouse that had been closed for many years, was renovated to accommodate their needs. We all pitched in. It was a great way to get to know the community.

The church at this time was a big part of our lives, which meant we had to make some adjustments. Firstly, primary was during the week, so getting the children to primary was made easier as the school bus driver, Bro. Johnson was a member of the church and lived in Calgary.

The children simply stayed on the bus and he dropped them off at the church after school and I stayed in town to pick them up when primary finished.

Sunday was a little different. Sunday school was in the morning, followed in the afternoon with sacrament. To be able to go home after Sunday school and have lunch and return would have been very tight.

Wayne and Sandia Gedalman - the family I mentioned earlier - came to our rescue. They invited us to have lunch with them and spend time with their family prior to going to sacrament. We thanked them for their offer but agreed that every other week we would bring the lunch.

Their children being somewhat of the same ages as ours got on well with Andrew, Tanya and Jason. Our friendship has continued even though we moved away.

By this time our friends Ruth and Harold who had introduced us to the church had moved to Ottawa, Harold being with the RCMP. We decided to visit them at Christmas. It was a wonderful reunion and we had a great time as we had never been further east than the Albertan border. While there we went to Montreal, visited the Olympic stadium, skated on the Rideau Canal and flew home in January 1977. Having enjoyed Ottawa and renewing our friendship with the Doerksen, we started planning for the year.

We had never been to General Conference so we decided to go in April 1977. It was wonderful walking around Temple Square knowing that most of the people were members. Jason's adoption had finally been approved so on May 14th he was baptized, and later we went to the temple in Cardston to be sealed for eternity with the family. In June my parents came for a visit and we took them on a trip to Kelowna and then Gull Lake. They returned to England on August 10th.

Chapter 17 | Back To The City

We started finding that driving back and forth to Calgary - whether it be for school, work or church - very time consuming. So we made the decision to return to live in Calgary. We enjoyed the 4th ward in Calgary so we decided to find a house in the ward boundaries.

A house on Wildwood Drive became available, just around the corner from our friends the Gedalman's so once again we prepared to sell up and move.

Not much happened in the next two years. Me working for myself was not working out so I had to close it down and acquired a position with a Mechanical Contracting Company as the Commercial Project Manager. I knew the owner as he had been with the company I worked for in Lethbridge.

My love of soccer was put to good use while living on Wildwood Drive. I was approached by some parents asking me if I would be willing to coach a 12-year old girls soccer team. Up until this time I had only been involved with young men. I said I was willing to give it a try if two other parents would assist me - which they agreed to. A notice went out giving the date and time the practice would take place. When the evening of practice arrived, about 15 girls showed up. My first part was to find out how much they knew about soccer and what foot they could kick with. By the end of the first practice, I knew I had my work cut out for me. I registered them in a league and arranged the purchase of shirts. Nothing better to boost the morale of a player than to give them a shirt.

We had about four weeks to get in shape.

Shape was not my concern. Getting them to realize that you had a position to play and couldn't just run after the ball wherever it went, was. To give all an opportunity to play on Saturdays you had to turn up for practice during the week.

The first game was a bit demoralizing to say the least. We lost - which was not unexpected - but 10-0 was more than some of the girls expected. The following weeks we practiced hard and by the middle of the season we were only losing by a few goals. We also scored goals much to the surprise of some of the girls.

Parents were then becoming my main concern. I mentioned at the start of the season that no practice attendance meant no playing (or only as a substitute) on Saturdays. Some of the parents felt this was unfair, but I wanted to give all a chance to play.

By the end of the season, we had actually won one or two games, but the main thing was the girls had a great experience and fun thrown in with it.

Chapter 18 | Caring For Others

It was on May 9th 1978, that a small little girl aged 3 years came into our lives as a special needs foster child. Her name was Patricia - we called her Patti.

She had been born prematurely, weighing under 2 pounds which had put a strain on her heart, so she required oxygen 24/7. Her parents could not look after her when she was born as both smoked and were finding it hard to give it up. We modified the bedroom so we could have an oxygen system installed for her. This meant she could also walk around the house with this 50-foot tube attached to her. We had a stroller fitted with an oxygen bottle so she could come out with us wherever we went.

On one such trip in 1978 we took her on holiday with us to Kelowna. This meant we had to have an oxygen system installed in our travel trailer and make arrangements to be able to replace empty bottles of oxygen in Kelowna. She was a joy to have around

Over the next year her heart became stronger. Now we were planning to move to Victoria from Calgary in December 1979. By the time it was for her to return to her parent she only needed to have oxygen while sleeping in her bed. Her parents by then had finally given up smoking and could care for her. When she was 10 years old her parents sent us a photo of her, but since that time there's been no more contact.

Chapter 19 | To See The Sea

Jenny and I had been to Victoria a few times, mostly in about April time when the winters in Calgary had started to get to us.

Victoria reminded us of England with its open ocean, sand beaches and a warmer climate.

So on July 20th 1979, we took a family trip to Victoria in a motor home. While there we asked Andrew, Tanya and Jason if they would like to move to Victoria.

Up until this time, while we had moved a lot, we had tried to stay in the same schools. Not always, but at least there had been less upheaval. This was going to be different. Andrew would be going into middle / high school and Tanya and Jason would still be in elementary school.

Meanwhile other plans had also been made. Jenny's Mum and Dad came to visit us on August 13th for three weeks. Lots was going on and a decision had to be made.

So, on September 28th 1979 on a Friday, Jenny and I flew to Victoria to look at the housing market. We had contacted a realtor prior to this and laid out our requirements. By Saturday night this realtor had shown us nothing that suited us, so the next day we went to the Quadra Chapel. It was the only chapel in Victoria at the time because the Victoria Stake Centre was still under construction. It ended up being Stake Conference that Sunday.

Following the conference, we spoke to a Sis Burbank, explaining our situation that we were out here looking at houses this weekend and would be flying back to Calgary in the evening. She introduced us to Chuck Loveday - a realtor.

After explaining our situation, he agreed to show us some houses. He explained he did not work on Sundays but would make an exception. By about 6.00pm we had seen a few which we thought would be fine, having taken in consideration the school locations.

We finally agreed to make an offer on a house on Tiffin Place because it was close to both Torquay Elementary and Lambrick Middle/High School.

Boarding our return flight to Calgary we heard that our offer had been accepted, that was great, the only problem being I could not remember much about the house. Chuck Loveday agreed to send us photos of the house and the surround area.

Upon arriving home, we told our plan to the children; Tanya was excited and Andrew and Jason were not sure. Our house in Calgary sold quickly and moving date was set for December 10th 1979.

Moving day arrived and having seen that the movers were nearly complete, we took off for Victoria. The weather was very cold with snow on the highway, especially on the mountain pass, but once over the mountains the weather improved and we arrived in Victoria on December 14th.

The movers promised delivery on December 16th (it being a weekend). Andrew, being very observant, had made a note before leaving of both the container numbers. They arrive as promised but with one correct container and another container...that was empty. Andrew pointed this out to them, and the driver was very indignant that a teenager would speak up to him. Well, you should have seen his face when the container was opened. How could anybody not tell the difference between an empty and full container! Especially when lifting them onto the flat deck. What happened to the container? It had been unloaded in Vancouver prior to coming to Victoria.

So, after all was unloaded, we had beds but no frames, a table with not chairs and various other parts of furniture.

The problem this all caused was I had already arranged to fly back to Calgary until Christmas for work, so I had to leave.

Thankfully the furniture arrived the Monday following and we settled into living in Victoria. Being by the ocean was uplifting for me. It brought me back to my childhood experiences. Looking around the harbours you cannot help but see all the boats.

So, guess what? We brought a boat. 24 feet long and slept six. It was great fun - if the ocean was somewhat calm. But just like our cabin back in Calgary, it had such limited use due to church on Sunday.

The children started school in January. Tanya and Jason going to Torquey Elementary school and Andrew going to Lambrick middle /high school. Both schools were within walking distance from home. Having felt we had left snow behind us, it was to our surprise that we woke up to snow within a few days of arriving. What was even more surprising, was the children were *given the day off school. Andrew complained that they did not do this in Calgary, but he made most of it, being the only people in the cul-de-sac with a snow shovel which had come with us. So out he goes and started snow clearing. Not sure if he got paid.*

That summer my parents came with Auntie Nina, so we took them on a trip up the coast. Due to not enough sleeping berths, we had to stop at locations that had motels so my parents and Nina could get a good nights rest. We docked in the marina's nearby.

In the summer of 1980 I was involved with the scouting program, so I volunteered to take the scouts out to Quadra Island for the weekend. They would camp on the Island and I would sleep in the boat. All went well until halfway through the night the boat listed to one side. Not knowing the reason, I got out of bed, and to my surprise, the boat was on dry land. I had not allowed for the tides, and therefore not let out enough anchor chain. So, I waited until about noon that day when the tide came back in to float again.

With the summer of 1981 coming and having not used the boat for some time, we sold it and with the money decided to build a swimming pool in the back garden. We thought we'd use it more. The pool was above ground, so a deck was built level with the rim of the pool. This allowed us to walk out of the living room sliding doors and almost dive directly into the pool. The code for pools was such that we had to have a fence 42" high around it - which was fine as the deck was tied into our house walls. To get the most out if it I manufactured a solar water heating system, made from ¾ inch tubing wound in coils installed under a clear plastic sheet which absorbed heat from the sun. It was located on our roof, facing the south, allowing the pool to be used for an extended period of time.

Having been a member of the Toastmasters organization in Victoria - and going to breakfast meeting once a week - I volunteered to teach the Toastmasters Principle's, (public speaking) to the elementary students at Torquay School. We met after school and it was great fun! Some of the students started out unable to stand up in front of a class, and then felt completely comfortable towards the end.

Chapter 20 | Run For My Life

One night in June 1982, while we all were seated around the table for supper, I happened to mention that Victoria had a marathon coming up in October. My running at this point had been limited to running around the neighbourhood for 30 plus minutes. I mentioned that 'I think I could run a marathon,' not realizing the distance was 26 miles. I think it was Andrew that said 'I don't think you can.' And that was the start of my many marathons. I signed up for the Victoria with the hope that by October I would be in good enough shape to complete it. By the middle of July, I felt I should try to see how far the race was. I knew it was 26 miles but how far are those 26 miles? The Victoria marathon in those days was two loops around downtown and the waterfront. Without telling anyone, one Saturday in July I drive to the starting area and started to run. Well, the outcome was I did one loop got back in the car before I passed out and spent 30 minutes recuperating before I was able to drive home. I found out that day, having done just half the distance, that 26 miles is a long way.

Well, October came, all hyped up with the other few hundred runners and completed the total distance in 3 hours and 38 minutes (approximately). At least I was not the last one - in fact many were behind me. I was only 39 years old...but feeling like 60.

This started my many years of running marathons, which over the next few years totalled about 12 or 13.

It was during this time that my attention was also drawn to triathlon's. I could ride a bicycle and running became easier, but swimming...that was a different story. Just like starting to train for a marathon, I drove into the pool headfirst for a triathlon, not aware of the total distance and multi training involved.

Swimming (the first part of the race), was 0.93 miles, the cycling 24.8 miles and then the running 6.20 miles.

Going to the pool I saw and met others training and noticed that the main stroke was the front crawl. My main stroke was the breaststroke. Much slower. So, I had to train myself by watching the others in the pool. Eventually I got the hang of it.

The Victoria triathlon was in July, the year I cannot remember but it started at Elk Lake with the swim, followed by the cycle to North Saanich and then running around Elk Lake.

It was a nice day and the time of the race start was 7.00am, with people starting to arrive at 6.00am. You would lay out your equipment on the ground in an orderly manner. Remembering that when you came out of the swim, you slipped on your cycling shoes and started to peddle like mad. I think the family came to give me moral support.

Could you imagine, over a hundred athletes running towards the water at the same time. I was in the middle - not the best place - quickly realizing that I should have been on the edge. Why? Because I was slow and swimmers started to swim over me - to which I felt like I was drowning. Eventually I was in the position where those around me swam at the same speed as I. I came out the water and there was Jenny taking a photo of me. The last one out. Never mind, it was the slowest of the three segments. I did finish with many behind me, vowing to improve upon my next race.

I completed many more, with at least two being with Andrew and Tanya. I then went on to complete a Half Iron Man in 1990 in Vancouver, swimming 1.2 miles, cycling 56 miles and running 13.1 miles. There I came in third for my age group.

Chapter 21 | Dear To Our Hearts

It was January 31st 1982 and while having had foster children in our home, a telephone call came for Jenny that a little girl was in need of a foster family. Her name was Juanita Jones. She was five years old (having been born November 24th 1976), and severely handicapped. She had been placed in Queen Alexandra Hospital for Children as her mother could not care for her.

The children fell in love with her the first time she came for a visit

For the next 16 years she became a part of the family. We were not able to adopt her as her mother would not consent to it, but she had little - if any - contact with her.

Jenny spent many hours with her social worker arranging treatments to help correct some of her disabilities. In the end, they were not handicaps at all. She became able to walk with the help of a prosthetic, feed herself and enjoy life with her brothers and sister. They truly were brothers and sister to her as far as we were concerned.

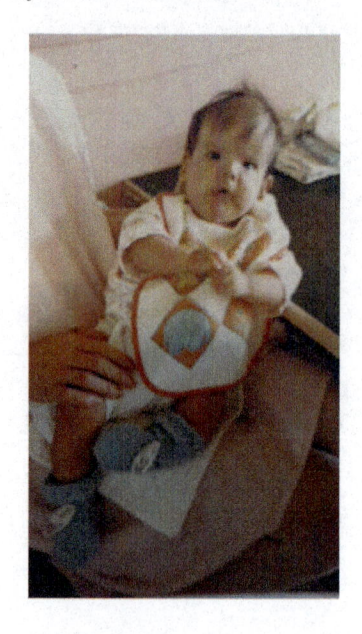

She came wherever we were able to take her, modifying our van so her wheelchair could be lifted into it. When walking became a problem, we had ramps constructed to wheel her into the house. She attended art classes at Garth Homer School, coming to church for awhile and attending primary.

When we moved to Kelowna in 1996 her health started to deteriorate and in January 1997 she passed away peacefully, returning to our Father in Heaven. Her funeral was held in the Victoria Stake Center and over 200 people whose lives she had touched, attended the memorial service which was conducted by Bishop Bob McCue.

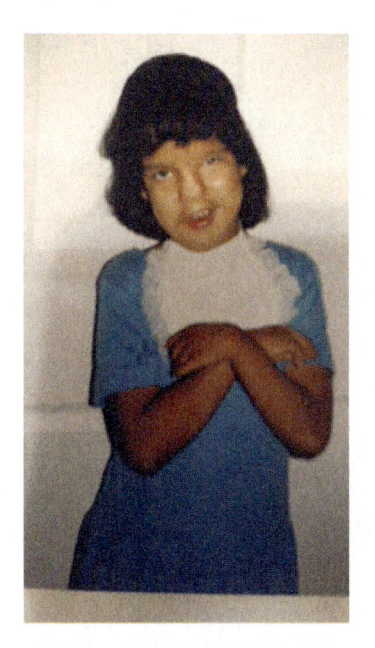

Moving forward in April 1998 we moved back to Victoria following Juanita's passing and purchased a house two doors up from the Barrie house we sold prior to moving to Kelowna. So, we still knew our neighbours.

We were really empty nesters now and started to look for ways to help others in life.

Chapter 22 | Kelowna Break

Going back a bit.

In 1996 we moved with Andrew, Shelley and their family to Kelowna. We bought a house and orchard on an acreage for us to live in. The house was on a slope and we livid on the upper floor, with Andrew and family in a walk out lower level. Yes, you guessed it. It needed to be renovated which we did while living in it.

The best part is that it had an outdoor swimming pool, 50 feet long by 25 feet wide, so the summers were spent as you can guess in the pool. One winter we dropped the water level allowing it to freeze over so we could use it as a skating rink.

Andrew had his business in a building on the property, and I worked in the apple orchard, spraying for bugs, pruning, and generally keeping myself busy.

I taught seminary for one year in the mornings to the youth living in Westbank, using part of Andrews office building as the classroom. It was fun until the winter came and snow had to be cleared most mornings prior to the start of seminary. Jenny prepared breakfast for the youth following seminary every two weeks on a Friday.

Church was in Kelowna on Glenmore road, so we had to travel over the bridge to attend it, as Westbank had no chapel at the time.

While teaching seminary I was called to serve as the 1st counselor in the YSA branch, with Brother Godfrey being the President. The YSA covered the whole Stake so on Sunday's the adults had travelled some distances, so we had a linger longer meal some Sunday's following services.

Chapter 23 | Sail Away?

At this point another adventure idea come into our minds. The year was around 1998 and we were still loving living by the ocean, so we decided to learn how to sail.

Why not? We had owned a power boat before, so the ocean was not something new to us. It was only the method of getting from A to B that would be slower. So off we go, each week to have sailing lessons. The theory part was understandable but the actual handling and maneuverability of the yacht was a different story

Well, we both passed the examination and now came the big test - taking a 25-35 foot sailboat out on our own.

Different story altogether.

After a few days (well weeks, should I say), we got this wild idea of going offshore. Also know as sailing the big ocean.

In the meantime, I had taken and passed the navigation examination so felt comfortable going into the big sea.

To prepare us for this phase, we needed to spend time sailing around the gulf island and staying overnight at sea.

Well..docking each night.

This where it all fell apart.

One day, while returning from a two or three day sail we were heading back to the Sidney Harbour and a storm arose. We were just passing Sidney Spit Island and my first mate - Jenny - requested that we sail into Sidney Spit and wait out the storm.

Although it was raining heavily, the sailing conditions were perfect and time to Sidney Harbour was only about 1 or 2 hours.

So I made the captains decision to sail on. Wrong decision as far as Jenny was concerned and she went down into the hull, leaving me to sail all alone. We arrived back safely but that put an end to offshore sailing for us, as Jenny would only sail if we could sail into harbour each night. This would be an impossible task as anyone would know that once you sail away from Vancouver Island the next land going west could be up to 19 or 20 days away. The adventure idea was good , just not practical at this point.

Chapter 24 | Next Phase

As the year 2000 came in I was contracted for one year to go and project manage a development in Vulcan Alberta. It meant that I would only be home Friday to Sunday. So, as not to leave Jenny on her own for too long, I rented an apartment rather that stay in a hotel, which would allow her to come and stay with me on some weekends - which in the end worked out very well.

Still, we felt we had to do something to help others.

Mexico came to our minds. Could we go there for a three-month period and do something? We started planning and in August 2001 we set off in our Nissan Quest van loaded to the roof line for Ajaji in central Mexico, just south of Guadalajara.

Having meet a couple - Jane and Mike - on a prior trip we at least knew someone when we arrived.

Below is my dairy of this trip which I hope with be of interest to you.

Draper's Caper's

Chapter 25 | Mexico Diary

August 20 | 2001

Today is the first day of our adventure. This is a trip we have dreamed of for many years, even though the destination has changed. At one time we were going to sail down to the Caribbean but that was a bit too adventurous for us, as you read before.

We left Victoria on a beautiful summer's day. As we looked out over the inner harbour we knew why we had loved our time there and knew we would be back to stay at a later time, good Lord willing. We took the Port Angeles ferry so we could miss travelling down the I5. Once off the ferry, we travelled down to Aberdeen and spent our first night there.

Keesha - our dog - has done surprisingly well with just a few low growls and the occasional bark. She travels extremely well, just sleeps most of the time.

August 21 | 2001

We were on the road by 9AM and travelled through some very picturesque countryside. As we had woken to rain (and it never stopped the whole day), we decided to just drive. An hour into our trip, just outside of Southbend, we came to a sudden stop behind a line of cars. After a short while, ambulances and fire trucks went whizzing by only to stop a few cars ahead of us. We sat and waited for over an hour. I got out to see when we would be able to go, only to see a horrific accident. Two cars were involved, the Jaws of Life had been used to remove the top of one car, and there were bits of car lying all over the road. A county officer told me that there had, in all likelihood, been a fatality so the road would not be cleared for another four hours. We decided to go back and find the detour they had set up. This took us on a logging road; thank goodness it didn't take very long. We lost over two hours. Never mind, we were relieved to be safe. You just don't know when your whole life will be turned upside down. One just assumes when you set off on a journey that you will reach your destination. We drove as far as Newport and passed some incredible coastline, but due to the pouring rain and fog we didn't stop .

August 24 / 2001

    We are now in Santa Rosa California - we arrived yesterday. Finally we have driven out of the rain and it is much warmer here but very humid. The temperatures are going to be rising from now on, 100 degrees or more as we head inland. Santa Rosa is in the wine country and is very pretty. We drove through vineyards and rolling hills and up until now we had been driving through rather run down looking places - logging towns and the like. Here it is much more prosperous. We went into the mall yesterday (our first one), and it was practically empty. We hope to reach the Monterey Peninsula, this being the last time we shall see the ocean for some time.

    Last night we phoned Brian, and Tanya was out celebrating Corey's birthday. It made us feel homesick. They have now got a settlement on the van so they are looking for a replacement.

Aug 26 / 2001

    The journey continues. I'm afraid I am no great lover of the U.S. Personally I think we have been brainwashed into thinking this country is the greatest. To me, Canada looks better every day. They have taken commercialism to the extreme. As we drove through L.A. and passed names like Sunset Blvd, Loma Linda, Malibu, Big Sur, Hollywood and Anaheim - all the names one associates with the GOOD life - I was impressed with the beauty of the place. There is no doubt it is drop dead gorgeous. I expected to see Robin Leach pop his head up and tell us about someone rich and famous. It is a dream that is sold to us, but in reality it is available to just a handful. The traffic jams went on for miles and we went through at 4.30pm on a Saturday afternoon. They have to deal with that every day. It made Vancouver look like a small country town.

We are now in Palm Springs (actually Cathedral Grove) and by 7am it was already 88 degrees and expected to reach 112f. We are staying close to our room or car or somewhere with air-conditioning. Poor Keesha cannot be left anywhere. As we drove through Palm Springs late last night (after a 10 hour drive) it looked like a pretty place. Today we will go have a look around. We will stay here for two days because we need to relax. One of the amazing things about making a trip like this is that you get to know exactly what is important to you, where your priorities are.

We just read something from a magazine that says somewhat of my feelings for this place, the thinking that money can take care of anything.

It reads

> **"Modern law has it that in England death is imminent, in Canada inevitable and in California optional. Failing hips can be replaced, clinical depression controlled, cataracts removed in 30 minutes but not even the health system can cure death."**

August 28 | 2001
Just a short drive this time, 4 hours. We drove through the desert.

One could imagine a cowboy coming over the hills. We decided to by-pass Phoenix and stay at Mesa as it is close to the temple.

We are at the Arizona Golf Resort, it is absolutely fabulous, and the incredible thing is that they only charged us $59. It is a large suite; huge in fact, there is a pool tennis courts exercise room. It was good to do some exercise, as all we've done in the last week is sit and eat.

Phoenix and Mesa are very attractive places, spotlessly clean and great to drive around. It is very hot still but there is a wind blowing which makes it somewhat more bearable.

Tomorrow we hope to attend the temple; we shall stay here for two days.

August 30 / 2001

After a 10-hour drive we finally arrived at San Antonio in Texas. We had planned to stop in Sonora but decided to just keep going. We would only be sitting in the hotel room all evening.

We watched the terrain change as we left Arizona into New Mexico and then Texas. We stayed last night outside El Paso, the drive from there to here was pretty bleak except the neat shapes of the mountains (if that's what they were). They rise up, then stop and are completely flat on the top. Hence the name Mesa. As we got closer to San Antonio it changed again and became quite green. It is pretty here.

We have found the trip quite stressful. We don't really know why because it is all such a wonderful adventure. We give thanks every night to our Father above for His safekeeping.

September 2 | 2001

 Yesterday was the most stressful day of them all. We crossed the border. We took the wrong turn at first after we had been given the green light to continue and found ourselves driving right on into Mexico! We hadn't acquired our tourist visas or car permits. We backtracked and found the building. As we entered the building there was a huge line up, which we joined. I noticed that people had different forms so decided to ask someone about it. That's when we found out we were in the wrong line. A young girl, Brittany, from Texas, came forward and offered to help; she was with her Mexican boyfriend. Thank heavens for her. She was great, taking us to where we had to start the process, even came back after a bit to see how we were doing. Then they let us back into the line up. We had a two-hour wait; it was nice talking to Brittany. Another fellow we talked to was on his way to San Louis Potosi and told us a little about the trip.

 We were finally out of there and on our way. It took us 8 hours on wonderful roads with beautiful scenery; we went through the San Madre Mountains into green valleys.

Homes on the road from Monterrey

There had obviously been a lot of rain in the last few days as there were huge puddles everywhere.

We found the Holiday Inn with little trouble. It is an incredible place, but costs us $200. We were so relieved to be here that we just decided to take it. To eat here is so cheap; our breakfast was less than $4 each. We are about to enter on the last leg of our journey to Lake Chapala; it should take us 4 hours. We understand the first part is going to be very steep and windy. We pray for the Lord's protection.

Sept 3rd

Lake Chapala

We are here (actually we arrived yesterday). It was just as windy and steep as they said it would be.

I was very nervous and relieved once we had gone through that part, the road did remain two lanes for half the journey so there were some nervous moments when we had to overtake. Also, we were down to just 8 Pesos and little gas by the time we arrived. We saw many people on the sides of the road selling fruit, pottery and other items, they were living in the tiniest little shacks, some could not even be called that. Some were made out of tree logs leaning, and a tarp hanging down in front. It is amazing when they come out of these places clean and neat, you wonder how they do it. In one village we went through, there were two girls waiting for a bus and they could've been walking down the streets of Vancouver, their clothes were so trendy.

It was lovely having Jane and Mike here to welcome us! We visited with them and they kindly invited us to dinner. After talking with them we do not think it's going to be as cheap to live here as we thought. So maybe we won't be able to stay as long as we thought, we will see.

We sat outside on the balcony eating breakfast this morning, it was so warm. It is now almost noon and very warm.

September 4 / 2001

Last night we took Jane & Mike out for dinner to La Bodega. It was a fun evening, but because of the amount they drank, the bill came to $100 - that was a bit of a shocker. We won't be doing that again.

It was rather noisy last night, the dogs were barking a lot. Keesha did not respond.

This morning we went and looked at some rental houses. We saw some wonderful properties; wishing we could have combined all the things we liked about each one. It seems to be between two places. One is a lovely house but a little secluded, we would be behind our own walls and probably not see anybody. It has fountains, huge rooms and a great garden for the dog.

The other place is in La Huerta, a fantastic, just-about-new place with everything we could possibly want. Only trouble is, we think it is mainly filled with gringos. I would feel completely safe there. We hope to go back and view the house tomorrow, and then we will make a decision. The shock for us is the price, almost double what we wanted to pay. There was one other house that would have been great as you are sharing the property with a Mexican family with delightful children. Only trouble was the house was so filled with the person's stuff, it would be like living back in Sidney again. It's never a straightforward decision that has to be made. But we are thankful that we do have a choice, as there is so very little to choose from. Ajijic is becoming an exclusive enclave.

September 9 / 2001

Well, we made the decision and took the La Huerta house and I feel like we are living the life of the rich!

Front / Side View 2001. 9. 15 13:02

  This is not what we anticipated when we came here. I had been thinking maybe something quite humble, no way you can call this place humble!

  Today we went to church, many of the same people we saw in February were still there, but we also met some new people, Donna & Craig Cramer from California. Actually, I just hung up the phone from talking to them, they are coming over tonight. The strange thing is that their situation is almost identical to ours. Craig has just retired from the government; they were going to put in their mission papers but decided they needed 6 months of R&R, so here they are. They are renting a house two blocks from us.

  Anyway, back to church. Because the bishop is away, the 1st. counselor in the bishopric conducted. He can only speak English, so we understood that part but the rest we could not understand. They did have a missionary who was trying to translate but he didn't understand enough to do a very good job. Priesthood was great, again all in Spanish, we at least had a manual to follow along with. Today we sat in the back of the chapel with the other gringos (that's where the headphones are for the translation), next time we are sitting up front, we didn't like the segregation.

It would be nice if I could've picked up the phone this afternoon to talk to the children. I shall be so glad once we are on to a long-distance plan. Also, it will be great once we are hooked up to the internet.

So far so good, this is the end of our first week, at the moment I don't even want to consider the thought of going back. Maybe I will feel differently a few months from now.

October 7 | 2001

We have already been here a month and the time has flown by.

We have just finished watching the Sunday conference sessions from Salt Lake, and then turn on the TV to hear that the attacks against the terrorist have commenced, we have to give thanks for what we have, and I wonder when it will all end.

This Monday is Canadian Thanksgiving and as I reflect, I truly have much to be thankful for. The knowledge that our children and grandchildren are safe and are cared for by all around is a real comfort.

This month of being in our own house has given us the opportunity to meet some wonderful people within the development and in Ajijic. Couples who have an interest in you and would come to assist if required. People here want us to have a good experience while we are here.

Jenny and I have just become involved with an organization called Niño's Incapacitados. On Saturday it required me to drive two people, one Mexican lady and a member of the group to visit a family, in another village around the lake, with handicapped children. I cannot explain the condition of the home only to say that the floor was part mud and concrete and the roof was made of corrugated metal. One child lay on cardboard on the mud floor and the other sat in a wheelchair. The girl in the wheelchair reminded me of Nita. I hope the organization will be able to help with some of the needs we observed. Time will tell.

Being able to communicate with our friends and family via e-mail has been wonderful. Listening to Conference on the computer has made the new computer worth all the money it cost.

Church has been a struggle as the membership is split 50-50 between gringos and mexicans. We listen to the talks on Sunday and are able to get the main theme of the talks from the little Spanish I have acquired. The bishop who has served for 3 years will be returning to the USA and Puerto Rico next week. We have been told that a recommendation has been submitted to Salt Lake. We hope that whoever it may be is Spanish speaking, as the local people need that. We will have to learn the language. The membership is 250 but only 30-50 come out on Sunday.

Another couple from the church arrived about six weeks prior to us. Their plans are so similar to ours, 12 months in Ajijic, then onto a mission.

Life in the village takes me back to my youth. We go shopping daily as it's nice to eat fresh produce. Everybody is relaxed and casual. Stores close between 2-4pm daily. Then stay open 6-9pm. As the roads within the village are cobble, walking can be awkward. You must watch your step. Look up then down. Down then up.

We are doing our missionary work the way we like best - by being friendly to all so that through our example the gospel light will shine through. When the question or religion is brought up, we answer to the person's satisfaction. The Mexican people go to church often and life revolves around the church because in most villages, the church is in the village square.

October 21 / 2001

    As I sit here my heart is filled with gratitude for the opportunity of being in Mexico. Since I last wrote we have met new friends and feel that we have settled into a lifestyle with some normal happenings.

    Each Tuesday morning, we assist with a horse-riding program for the handicap.

Children from Ajijic and the surrounding areas are brought to an area where the gringos take them on a 20-minute ride and following the ride, a local massage therapist works on the circulation systems of their bodies. A Mexican stable provides the horses. The children enjoy it so much. It reminds me of Nita as she was in a similar program in Victoria.

Yesterday the missionaries had an open house at the church. The stake missionaries arranged it. The only problem is that they do not advise the Bishop of all their intentions. We fed 40 missionaries pancakes and fruit at 10.00am. (they had told us 9.00am). So we waited patiently. Following which the missionaries had a meeting and left the church to go to various areas to invite people to the church at 5.00pm. At 3.00pm we fed the missionaries on their return. Jenny and some other sisters made up 12 large loaves into sandwiches. Our responsibilities were to arrange a room - which serves as the relief society, kitchen and baptismal area - into a celestial room. We had to find all the items to do so. Well, we managed to round-up enough items. The missionaries had a TV set up on the grounds outside plus a speaker system. Following the open house there was a baptism. As we did not stay the complete time we assumed all went well. When the young missionaries make up their minds to do something, nothing stops them. The interesting part is that there is no budget, (attendance is only 60 members so budget allowances are small) and it is expected that the gringos will pay for everything...which we did.

The rains have stopped and for the last week the sun has shone. I am still having problems with the Spanish language. Jenny is doing much better. Exercising three times a week is helping me get back into shape and is helping my back.

October 25 /2001

Last Sunday we had a stake priesthood meeting in Guadalajara at 5:30pm. We managed to get nine priesthood to attend. You must realize that very few Mexican members have cars, so it is up to the gringos to provide transportation. We had two vans. One brother came as the translator. He sits behind us and we can get the message. The stake president does not mix his words. He told them that one evening the stake centre had the lights left on, garbage around the *outside, and books in disarray. The main theme of the meeting was for the members to have a 72-hour food supply. The list handed out was different from the requirements in Canada.*

While talking to Andrew, he informed me that he has been called to the state high council. He mentioned that it would be nice if I could set him apart. This has been a hard decision. I would love to be able to, but being on a limited budget, and the flights being $800, we feel that we would not be able to attend. Jenny & I realize that this is going to be an ongoing struggle every time the family has a church calling or advancement - the need or want to be there. Just hope that the spirit prompts the person, as if I would have given it.

November 3 /2001

We have just returned from a wonderful week at Barra de Navidad. To see the ocean was most invigorating. We went with our friends Mike & Jane. We took the toll road out to the coast. Our first stop after leaving Ajijic was Colima. This is the state capital of Colima. The town is beautiful and clean. We admired the government buildings and the church.

Government Office-Colima 2001. 10. 29 11:04

Both are located around the town square. Prior to entering the town, we viewed the fire volcano from the highway. The steam or smoke is continually coming out of it. Due to time restraints, we did not get too close. There is also a cold volcano. This volcano in the winter will have snow on it. We left after lunch and travelled to Manzanillo, then onto Barra de Navidad. The weather was perfect, and the sand by mid-afternoon could not be walked on with bare feet. It had not changed since our last visit in February. To get a better idea you will need to view the photos.

All agreed we needed to see the ocean. As much as we like Ajijic, the ocean still has a strong pull, although the temperatures in summer - together with the humidity - may be unbearable. After one night we went around the bay to Melaque. Similar beach but nicer to swim in. While at Barra we visited some property and building lots. Mike would like a place by the sea. They are sailing fans, so would like a boat to be able to sail on weekends. By the way, it takes only 4.5 hrs. to travel to the ocean. Our return trip was on the free road. Because the rainy season has just stopped, the scenery was wonderful. The fields have pineapples, sugar cane and mangos growing. The only drawback to the free road, are the TOPES. If you see this sign, slow down to crawl. The Topes are speed bumps in the road. If you drive over at any speed above a crawl, you will lose the underside of your car. Every village has at least two, usually three. We are looking forward to our next trip which although not to Barra it will be to the coast. This will be to pick up Tanya and family and to stay at Sayulita.

Because of the high altitude of Ajijic, (5000 ft.) it is starting to get cold in the evenings. May have regretted not bringing warmer clothes.

November 1-2/01 are celebrated in Mexico as the Days of the Dead. The families visit the graves, laying beautiful wreaths and flowers on the grave. They also bring the deceased person's favourite food and eat it at the grave. The local priest conducts a service. Nov.1/01 is for children that have died, Nov.2/01 is for adults. Couples in our complex have adopted the grave of a lady from the USA who died in 1990. We went with them during the day to lay flowers on her grave. The Mexican treat this as a happy time, with fireworks and parties. See the photos.

Corona-Wreath of Flowers

November 16 /2001

Time seems to pass so fast. Only four weeks till Tanya and family arrive. Jenny is becoming involved with the Orphanage and I have been asked to investigate the membership records for the Barrio Ajijic. I also still help with the handicap horse riding program on Friday mornings. We seem to have more volunteers than children. This may change.

The other day while walking on the lakefront, I seemed to have gone back 70 years, for there, in front of me, was a farmer ploughing the field (or should I say the lakebed). What was so amazing was the plough. It was a single blade on a wooden shaft and was pulled by two horses. He controlled the horses by a rope around his shoulders. Next time on the lake I will take my camera. The vegetables being planted looked like zucchini. Irrigation is through troughs on either side of the plants. The lakebed is also used as the grassing grounds for cattle, probably 50 –60 head. For these people this is their income, which may seem to us meager, but is sufficient for their needs.

How are we finding this experience being in Ajijic? The big change is being able to slow the pace. No need for a watch, as most activities never start on time. By looking at the sky you begin to tell the time. Language is always a problem for me, but I have decided to proceed at my own pace. Jenny has mastered it very well and is having lessons at the beginners level. With Jenny's help I will study under her, until I feel comfortable taking lessons - which I will benefit from.

The church is still struggling. The Bishop has gone back to Utah, as his wife is sick. He advised the Stake President in March that he would be doing this, but the stake did not release him. The counselor, who speaks no Spanish, is holding it together. We understand that names have been submitted but no decision forthcoming.

The last meeting to which the stake president came, he mentioned he felt the ward was sick. Strange thing to say, realizing that six months had passed since the bishop advised of his departure. Even so I enjoy going to church and will continue to assist in whatever way possible. From this experience you realize what good training we receive from leaders in Canada.

November 23 /2001

 Today we delivered the groceries to the orphanage. The children were in school but when we arrived three boys appeared to help unload. The lady responsible for the kitchen, Maria, was so pleasant and appreciative. Although we will not be able to attend the Christmas party at the orphanage (because we will be at the coast with Tanya), we have volunteered to shop for the food and deliver it. As a note, Tanya is collecting clothes in Victoria so that we can provide additional gifts for the children that are not able to spend Christmas with relatives. Approximately. 20 children.

 Ajijic has had two parades this week. Tuesday was Revolution day, which is a holiday to remember the 1920 revolution. The parade was at 10:00am, following which they performed in the village square.

 Wednesday was the start of the San Andres six-day celebration. San Andres is the saint of Ajijic.

 The parade was at 5:00pm. and consisted of about 15 floats depicting the life of Jesus on the earth. starting with his birth. If only this could be done in Canada, but with a society not willing to accept any religious performance in public, Canada is losing out. The children participating in the parade really took it seriously. The standard of living may not be as high, but in our eyes, they are far above us spiritually. We have seen children when passing their churches make the sign of the cross.

Jesus and Fishermen

I was just called away from the computer as a cockroach was chasing Jenny.

December 1l 2001

The celebrations for San Andres week have been completed. It's hard to explain what activities take place, as there are so many. Needless to say, the fireworks that start at 6:00AM and go for about 15 minutes in the morning, together with the church bells will not be missed. Each day a different occupation, i.e. contractors, lawyers, doctors, storekeepers, etc. will sponsor the fireworks and activities. I will just cover the evening we went to the village square. It was about 8:30pm and we noticed that the girls were circling the square one way and the young men the other. Every so often a boy would shower a girl with confetti. We had been told of the activity but had not seen it played out. It was amusing to watch. The midway consisted of about four ride units and small enough to be erected in the narrow streets. At 10:30 or thereabout, the 'Castillo' would be started. This is a vertical firework display. It starts at the bottom and each level is lit. Takes about 20 minutes.

As we prepare for Christmas and the arrival of Tanya and family, the excitement is beginning to show within Jenny and I. We went to a market in Guadalajara and bought a tree (artificial) and decorations. The city is not decorated out as was Victoria, but the stores have all the items for the family and children's needs. This Christmas reminds me of the time we spent Christmas in the Caribbean. We would sure like to have all the families here with us.

December 19 l2001

Christmas time has arrived. We have returned from P.V. and a week with Tanya and family at Sayulita. The children have been wonderful to see. The weather was a little overcast but warm. Sayulita is a small fishing village north of P.V. and has great surfing. The children so easily adapt to their surroundings. Corey and Jeff made friends with the maid's children and with a little help were able to communicate. Jeffrey gave the boy a tee shirt with Canada across the front. While in Sayulita the celebration of the Virgin of Guadalupe took place. The whole village came out to participate. The highlight was the fireworks, which the children did not see as they were so tired from their journey.

The children are in awe at the sites they see. Having come from clean Victoria, this is definitely a culture shock.

December 22 I 2001

Yesterday we took the gang to Libertar Market. What an experience. Three floors of every item you can think of. This was the first experience of Christmas the family had seen. The girls felt closed in as all the people were pushing. Most of the time Tanya or Brian carried them.

Christmas is a time to remember the birth of our Saviour. Mexico, with its deep religion, celebrates it more than we do in Canada. Not many signs of Santa Claus, more of a scene of the nativity. Even the poorest of families have a crèche. The village of San Antonio reenacts the travel of Joseph and Mary to Bethlehem each night from Dec. 18-24/01. At 6:00 each night, they set out from a different house in the village and travel to the church, knocking on doors on the way, requesting a room until they reach the church where a room is found.

December 23 I2001

Last night the ward had a Christmas party. All I can say is that the children had a wonderful time. Never worry about the language barrier. The children can converse well with hand signs. Attendance was about 70. Food was Mexican style-Tamales, together with drinks that had to have been loaded with calories. So good. The climax was the breaking of the Pinates. Eight in all. Full of candies, oranges and peanuts.

Today church only had sacrament meeting. The primary was in charge and gave a wonderful presentation through stories and songs. The children tried to understand. The missionary sat behind and translated. The primary gave out baskets full of candies at the end. Each basket was made of peanuts and coated in clear lacquer. I feel that for Jeffrey and Corey this will be remembered for many years.

December 25 /2001

  The highlight of Christmas was the eve before (24th). We decided to celebrate the Mexican way, so we had Christmas dinner on the evening of the 24th. Then we went to San Antonio to participate in the posada at 6:00pm. Although hard to explain, the message is that of the birth of our Saviour. You travel through the village from the main house and at designated homes the story of the birth is retold, and a song is sung which I have written below. It translates into the request to stay at the house, but just as Mary and Joseph were denied accommodation, so the children are denied entry. The children sing as they walk through the streets. It gives you the feeling of Christ's birth more so than I have ever had in Canada, other than going to the nativity pageant.

  Today the children opened their presents in the morning and this afternoon we are going to the lake which some members of the church we know, to water ski and relax.

  I think the children have really enjoyed this time. By the way, the sky is blue and 86 degrees.

The song   (first verse by the men, second by women.)

        APUERA
        EN EL NOMBRE DEL CIELO
        OS PIDO POSADA
        PUES NO PUEDE ANDAR
        MI ESPOSA AMADA

        NO SEAIS INHUMANOS
        TENGAN CARIDAD
        QUE EL DIOS DE LOS CIELOS
        SE LOS PREMIARA

        VENIMOS CANSADOS
        DESDE NASARETH
        YO SOY CARPINTERO

DE NOMBRE JOSE

POSADA TE PIDE
AMADO CASERO
POR SOLO UNA NOCHE
LA REYNA DEL CIELO

MI ESPOSA ES MARIA
ES REYNA DEL CIELO
Y MADRE VA ASER
DEL DIVINO VERBO

DIOS PAGE SENORES
SU GRAN CARIDAD
Y LOS COLME EL CIELO
DE FELIZIDAD

TODOS JUNTOS

ENTREN SANTOS PEREGRINOS, PEREGRINOS, RESIVAN ESTE RINCON.
QUE AUNQUE ES POBRE LA MORADA, LA MORADA
OS LA DOY DE CORAZON.

Enero 12 /2002.

 A new year has started, and Tanya and family have returned to Victoria. I cannot cover all the activities, but needless to say, they were numerous. They experienced going to the markets, sightseeing in Guadalajara, and riding a horse and buggy around Guadalajara.

 On January 1st we all travelled to Sayulita for the last week. Having already spent a week there, the children were completely at home. Being able to surf, swim and roam the streets at night without any worries made the experience worthwhile.

 We also were able to experience a Mexican wedding. The bride and father walked from their house to the church. Following behind were members of the wedding party and bringing up the rear was a band. It gave you the feeling that the whole village was part of the festivity.

If one thing I hope the grandchildren have gained from this trip is a better understanding of life in Mexico. The culture, simpleness and love shown to them by encountering Mexican families and their everyday activities.

We just heard that the 11th grandchild has arrived. Lucus Cole Draper. Michelle and baby are doing fine. First child we have not been at the birth but realize that this may be the case from now on.

How quiet the house is. We must start getting back into our routine.

Jenny and I have made the decision to stay in Mexico for another year. It has been a hard decision as going on a mission was our original goal. We have realized that being here for only six months would only give us a start in giving help to the organizations we have become involved in. It also means that we can come back to Victoria and Kelowna and visit with family and attend special functions, which going on a mission would not let us do.

The church is in need of leadership and although we don't want to give the impression that we have all the answers, we are able to assist.

Jenny enjoys going to the orphanage, and working with the ninos within the village.

Coming back and having said goodbye to Tanya and family, we have received hugs and kisses from the friends we have made here, which make us feel part of the community.

January 27 /2002.

One item not mentioned is the dog, Pedro. The children in Sayulita befriended him. We promised the grandchildren that we would bring him back to Ajijic if he was still around when we left Sayulita. As you can guess he was. Keesha and him have accepted each other so all is well. Time will tell.

Febrero 2 /2002

The week has gone by so fast, but at the same time exciting. Jenny and I have become involved in a school renovation project. The work involves upgrading to a chemistry classroom in a middle school (grade 7-9). Because of the condition of the classroom the students do not study chemistry. The local parents and North Americans are all pitching in. Local merchants are donating materials and the school raised $3200.00 US by having a Mexican fiesta at the school. The money raised will be used to pay for any items not donated.

Jenny is helping by arranging to have clothes sent down from Canada. The children must have school uniforms, otherwise they cannot attend school, and this may be the only clothes they have. School supplies are also needed i.e., pencils, erasers and books. We will see what we can do.

We spent two nice days with our friends Jim and Pat. We drove them to Metemela, a village up in the mountains. Reminds you of a Swiss village, the following day spent in Tonala for market day. Pat was looking for some special drinking glass.

Fruit is so plentiful year-round. One fruit, raspberries, are grown just outside Ocotepeque and while we were there bought a box full. What is interesting is that the fruit was being packaged to be shipped to England. Because of the heat and cold variations, the fruit is under a poly cover, somewhat resembling a greenhouse without the sides.

I had a wonderful experience this week. While walking the dogs down by the lake I heard this noise. The only way to describe it was like a windstorm. I looked into the sky and all I could see was this black mass, about 30 feet wide and three to four hundred yards long. Upon closer observation I realized that it was a flock of small birds flying in mass. The noise was their wings vibrating against the air while in flight. Although I was not able to photograph it, the sight was incredible. The following day I again was walking the dogs and noticed that the bushes growing in the lake had this black top to them, which I had not noticed before. At that moment somebody shouted. The black top turned out to be birds for they all took to flight. There had to be hundreds, possibly thousands. The sky became a black mass once again.

It is these wonderful sights that make it so enjoyable to be here.

We were able to celebrate on Martes, the 54th birthday of our friend Jim from St. John, Newfoundland. With his wife Pat they are down here for the month of Enero. All of us (eight) spent the evening at Tio's, a restaurant just across from our house. The highlight was having Jim break a piñata, which was hanging in the street outside the restaurant. Pat, his wife, just could not stop laughing. A good time was had by all.

Having decided to stay another year, we have been able to negotiate a reduction in our rent for signing a one-year lease.

With this accomplished Jenny has decided to plant some plants in the garden to give a more homelike feeling. Plants are so reasonable we do not mind providing them. So instead of looking at the green grass, we can look at a triangle flowerbed in front of our patio. Jenny would like a fountain. That may not come to pass.

Febrero 24 / 2002

Today we had a very spiritual sacrament, not because Jenny and I spoke but because of the feeling one felt in the chapel. We had 60 in attendance. This is a great improvement from the 32 last September.

We spent Tuesday evening at the chapel. It was mutual night, so all the families were invited to attend. Games and sports for the youth. As always, refreshments followed.

The school project got into top gear on Saturday as 12 hombres attended to help sand chairs and resurface the counters. The hombres promised to come next Sabado. We wait and see.

Spanish lessons are proving to be a challenge. We will overcome.

Having signed a one-year contract on the house we are set to continue life here.

It is interesting how you can slip into the daily routine so easily.

Last week we had an unusual windstorm. I say unusual in that we usually only get rainstorms but this one was from the east and lasted all night. Upon awakening we welcomed the sight of leaves completely covering our garden and dogs that were freaked out. It took most of the day to clear up the mess. Fortunately, our neighbours had rakes for us to use. First work we have done for some time.

Marzo 25 | 2002

Had not realized that a month had passed since I last wrote in the journal.

What has happened?

Eileen and Peter Bevan came for two weeks. We met them at the coast and then came back to Ajijic.

Eileen was able to gather some wonderful items to give to the niñas, i.e., makeup and clothes. The makeup will be given to the niñas who are excelling at the grades they are in. They cannot believe that people outside of Mexico would provide them with items like this.

The school project continues to progress. All the chairs have been painted and we are in the process of reinstalling the classroom to its original conditions.

The padres are only able to help two to three hours a week on a Saturday, the fun in doing this project is reflected in their eyes. All the hombres and mujers have children in the escular.

Painting Chairs — 2002. 3. 2 16:18

Marzo 22 / 2002

It is Good Friday here. How wonderful to see the whole village become part of the reenactment of the crucifixion. The church in the square has been transformed into a replica of Pontius Pilate's palace on the front, with actors portraying the various people at the crucifixion. Following the trial, the actor portraying Jesus is led away through the village streets, up the hills above Ajijic and then crucified. The street leading up to the site is decorated.

The other side of this weekend is that it's a major Mexican holiday. The lakeside is turned into a holiday town. Mexican families (note families), come to the lake and swim, water ski and have a very enjoyable time. One must see it to understand the enjoyment that is gained during this time.

Could you imagine the Easter message being reenacted on the streets of Victoria?

Marzo 24 I 2002

It is Palm Sunday, which marks the start of Holy week. The road leading up to the roman catholic church in Ajijic was strewn with green alpha to represent the palms laid on the path that Jesus took on his entry to the city. The priest will lead the procession, with Jesus bringing up the rear. On Thursday they will reenact the betrayal of Jesus by Judas Iscariot. Friday the crucifixion and Sunday the resurrection. The whole village becomes involved in the Easter tradition.

Marzo 31 I 2002

Today at church was fast Sunday, 62 in attendance, and although I was not able to understand all the testimonies the spirit was there. It was Easter Sunday.

I had translated my thoughts into Spanish but was unable to give it as my pronunciation is still very poor, and Jenny felt I needed more practice.

Abril 23 I2002

We are sitting in the airport in Los Angeles awaiting our flight to Vancouver. We will be visiting our family and friends for the next five weeks.

So much has happened since my last entry. My mother has been in and out of hospital twice, and at present is home in stable condition. I pray for guidance as to whether I should go home to England. Once in Canada I will assess the situation.

On Abril 21/02 I was sustained as first counselor in the bishopric of the Ajijic ward. To say I feel inadequate would be an understatement. Having a limited Spanish vocabulary, I feel that my reason for this call is to assist with the administration of the ward. The new bishop is very spiritual but lacks the depths of church administration. In the setting a part of this calling I was given a blessing of the gift of tongues. With this calling comes the feeling that this may be our mission. Jenny has been a great strength to me, and I love her very much. I am always reminded of the song: because I have been given much I too must give ...

Mayo 28 / 2002

Ever had the feeling that time is flying by? We have just returned from Kelowna and Victoria having spent a wonderful time with our children and grandchildren.

The first week was spent with Andrew and family. On Sunday Abril 28/02 Jenny and I were able to be in attendance as Andrew bestowed the Aaronic Priesthood upon Zak and Alex. I feel so close to the twins. They have a wonderful spirit about them. Rachel is growing so fast into a nice young girl.

Each day we walked to school with the children, and on Viernes (Friday) we attended a presentation in Alex and Zaks class on Japanese culture. I don't think the boys enjoyed the food samples given out.

On to Victoria. How Tanya manages with homeschooling and the sports activities I shall never understand. Needless to say, we were very welcomed. I tried to attend the boy's baseball games and training for water polo. There is a good feeling within the home.

On Viernes May 10/02 Jason and Tanya's families all travelled to Osoyoos for a family get together.

Shelley had arranged for four units in a motel on the lakeshore. The weather was very cooperative. Every family pitched in with the meals with one family taking charge of the evening meal. On Sunday we attended the Branch in Osoyoos and accounted for 30% of the attendance.

June 11 / 2002

Jenny and I spent the afternoon at a special needs school in Chapala. The school opened in April 2002 with 20 children and young people. It reminded us so much of the facilities that Nita went to. The reason for the visit was to see if we could be of assistance to the school. We were told that the school had equipment i.e. desk and speaker systems to be assembled. It also turned out to have a need for a considerable amount of school supplies. The big surprise was that the school has been operating since April without electricity. It should be turned on next week. Jenny wishes to become involved with the therapy of the children and is going to work with the doctor as to the type of therapy need. Paul Mireault, a massage therapist from Canada, is *going to give Jenny some instructions on the basic therapy needs also. Some of the children also come to the horse-riding program on Fridays.*

June 16 / 2002

I am trying to settle into my calling as 1st counselor in the Ajijic ward. Today was Ward Conference and the stake auxiliary came in full force. Jenny has been called as president of the young women's. Her 1st counselor has some English and hopefully will be able to assist with the language barrier. Jenny came out of her meeting wondering what she had involved herself into. The bishop came by following church and with my assistance set her apart. The stake president in sacrament spoke of the spirit that can overcome the language barriers. The missionaries came for lunch and I had them write out the whole sacrament program in Spanish. We will see how I do next week. The spirit will have to guide me.

The rains have come; in fact, today we had hailstorms.

The hills are turning green, and the dust is going. The dogs are petrified of the thunder and lighting. We bring Pedro in at night.

Junio 30 | 2002

    Today was a little disappointing. The church had made arrangements for the satellite broadcast of the dedication of the Nauvoo Temple at the stake centre, but halfway through the service the satellite went down. We found out that the sun had sent out a magnet heat ray and knocked out the satellite to all Central and South America. Hopefully we may be able to see the broadcast at some later date.

Julio 1 | 2002

    We were just at the coast with our friends Mike & Jane for a week. The weather was wonderful but oh so humid. We rented a house on the hillside overlooking the Sayulita bay. This time of the year the waters are calmer, so you are able to swim easily. We walked to other beaches around the bay and enjoyed the even calmer waters. On one of our walks, we suddenly came upon a rustling sound on the path in front of us. Upon further observation, we noticed hundreds of land crabs scurrying through the leaves and brush off the path. Each grab was about 4 inches across, having black backs with yellow legs. This was the first time I had seen so many crabs. Travelling through the countryside this time of the year is very beautiful. The rains have turned the landscape into various shades of green.

View from House in Sayulita 2002 7 3 7:17

Julio 15/ 2002

    Well, we are now living in a house without a gated community. The area is La Floresta and is a very nice area in Ajijic. The house belongs to a member of our church who has had to go back to the United States because of medical problems. We have had to pack and dispose of all their clothes and personal effects. To say the least it has been a tiring time for Jenny, as she has had to do most of the packing. It feels like a home, not a rented house. It has a lovely garden. Just the right size...with a fountain. The family in the states wishes to sell the house but the market is very slow so they are holding off until the winter. Jenny loves potting around and has the gardener cutting back the bushes. She is in her element.

    We had the opportunity on Saturday Julio 13/02 to attend the graduation ceremony of a sister from the church. She is 62 and has travelled from Chapala to Jocotepec, two villages up the lake, every Saturday for I don't know how many years, taking the course to graduate with a teaching degree. She was so pleased that we attended.

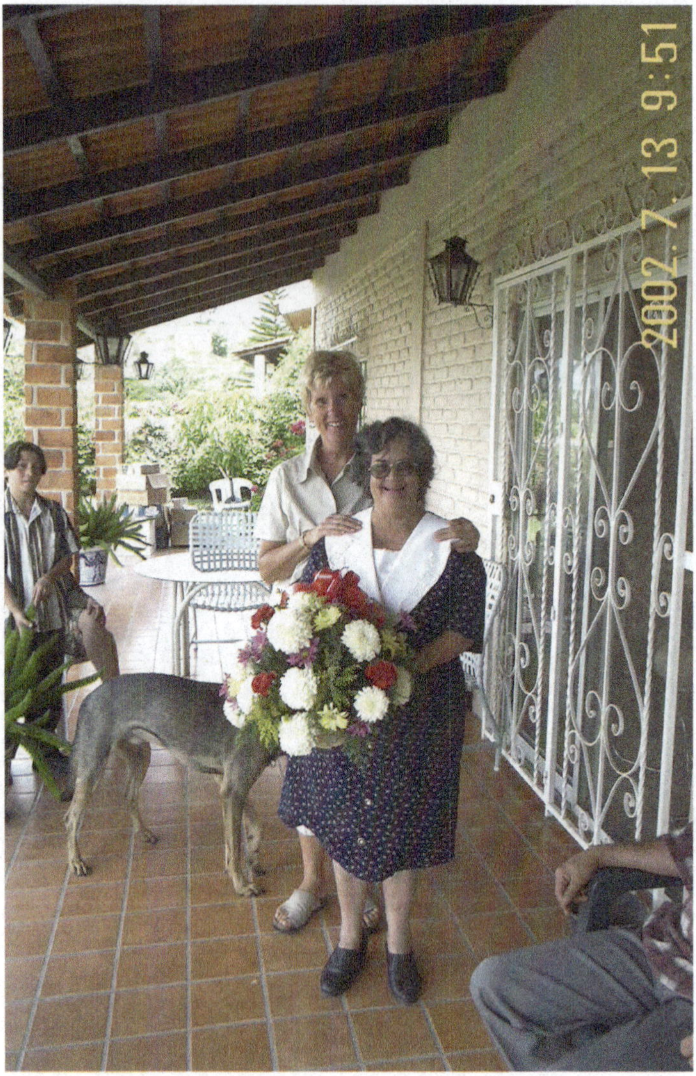
2002. 7. 13 9:51

Julio 17 / 2002

Today, Jenny had Veronica and Anna, two young women from the church, come over to the house to work on their skirts. This is a project to start the girls on their personal progress certificate. The girls have never made a skirt and I'm not sure if they have ever used a sewing machine. It may take many weeks to complete. Sister Bullock provided the sewing machines.

Veronica at the sewing machine 2002. 7. 17. 15:24

Agosto 8 / 2002

When people say 'what do you spend your time doing,' I feel that I need to think about what free time we have. We may not be on a mission from the church, but we do try to spend time working with the members within the ward, and within the community. By being an example, we hope others will receive a good feeling about the church.

These last two weeks have been most fulfilling. We started on July 28/02 when the bishop had to interview each youth for a conference. This may not seem too arduous but in this case, we had to find out if they were worthy to enter the temple as well. It's so disappointing when a young man admits to drinking and drugs and cannot go because we felt he would influence the others, and is not worthy. Eight youth are worthy to go.

Each Monday, I spend the morning preparing and submitting the tithing to the church in Mexico City. Firstly, I must find the ward financial clerk. He is inactive, but I know where he works. He is always willing to come to the church and do tithing. I always encourage him to come to church, but his family wants him to spend time with them on Sunday.

The afternoon is spent installing a telephone cable and outlet in a friend's house. Non-members, Mike and Jane, but wonderful people.

Tuesday, and time for Spanish lessons. Nelly is a member, and the person I mentioned earlier that graduated. I try, but only understand about 20% of what she is saying. Jenny does much better. Anyways, it's fun and we have a good laugh over my accent.

The afternoon finds me at the blue school, located in Chapala. This school is for handicapped children. School is out but the director has a problem. When it rains the water comes under the doors into the office and classroom. My project is to install three door sweeps to elevate the problem. Jenny hopes to work with a doctor at the school to give therapy to the children in September. In the evening Jenny and I take Tia Chi for 1 ½ hours. It is very relaxing.

The youth on Wednesday have to be transported to Guadalajara, because I have to go in on Thursday to assist in the temple, Bro. Smith volunteers to take the youth.

Instead, I go to my school project in Ajijic in the afternoon and test out all the plumbing. It must be completed by Agosto 19/02. School is back in that day and the chemistry room is needed.

Thursday is a special day. I spent the morning visiting the members of the ward with the English-speaking missionary. I am getting a better feeling for the church members. We are concentrating on the families with youth. If we can get the youth interested in coming perhaps the parents will be more willing to come on a regular basis. Following our visits, the missionaries come for afternoon lunch.

In the afternoon the bishopric travelled to Guadalajara to assist the youth doing baptisms for the dead. I am asked to assist. It's interesting, listening to the baptismal prayer in Spanish. I try to memorize it, but they speak so fast. I then proceed to the confirmation room and assist with the names. This is interesting as some of the names are English and as the person is being confirmed I say the name in English. We arrived home late in the evening.

Friday is shopping day. Mike, Jane, Jenny and I travel back to Guadalajara. Mike drives as I have driven enough. We do this outing once a month. Today we are looking for a dress material shop. Jenny wants to make some clothes. The material shop has every type of material you would want, and Jenny finds just what she needs. A trip to Guadalajara is not complete unless we visit Costco and Sam's Store. As this is Friday, we agreed to eat out. We have heard of this Argentine restaurant on Ave Vallarta, so set out to find it. Well, the meal was fabulous but pricey. This we do only on special occasions next time.

Saturday finds me back at the school. I have contacted a member of the church who is coming to help finalize the last countertop. The padre who had agreed to assist has let me down so often I have given up on him. Jenny has told me that the students will initially look after the classroom, but it will soon fall into disrepair. I feel this may be the case but at least it will start operational. I will never see the outcome.

Fast Sunday and I have to conduct. I have the program written out in Spanish and English. I have practiced with Nelly the previous Tuesday, but still rely on Junior, (that's his name) the 2nd counselor to assist. Give me six months. The spirit is there today. Fourteen members bore their testimonies, with 44 members in attendance. We hear through the grapevine that some Mexican members feel uncomfortable having to go to the bishop with personal matters and have his second counselor be in attendance to translate. He feels the same but until there are worthy High Priests to fill the bishops position, we cannot change. The missionaries brought an investigator, which they do most Sundays. I learned afterwards that she would like to join but her husband is abusive and possessive, so she must leave the casa when he is not looking. Not the ideal way to be active in the church. We will see how it turns out.

You can see from this that we have plenty to fill our weeks but are grateful for the opportunity to be here.

Agosto 13 /2002

What a satisfying day. Firstly, the school project is completed. The remaining work will be completed by the school district. It was not until I reviewed the original photos did I really get a feeling for the transformation that took place. I have told Jenny that I will not return to the school as it may not be maintained in its present condition for too long. At least it started out operational.

Rear to Front. (completed)

This evening we attended a concert put on by the Houston Children's Chorus. The music and song was wonderful. The children in the front row wore clothes from the heritage they came from.

The choir was founded in 1989. (www.houstonchildren.org) It involved over 250 children, ages 9 through 14, by annual audition. The choir sings from memory all types of music and performs more that 75 concerts per year for over 750,000 people. They have performed for the presidents of the United States on thirteen occasions. The Choir has also performed concerts in New Zealand, England, Vatican, Hong Kong, but this was the first time in Mexico. All the members have to pay their own way. The choir does have corporate sponsor's to offset some of the costs. The children are housed with Mexican families while in Ajijic. Their biggest sponsor was Enron, the now defunct electrical company.

The only downside to the concert was that at the beginning, the Canada national anthem was played. All the Canadians stood and the American stayed seated. When the American anthem was played following the Canadian, they all stood. Reiterates my feelings for the Americans.

The time is 11:20pm on August 20th and Jenny and I were both getting ready for bed. The telephone rings and Andrew is calling to tell us he has been called as the new Bishop of the Kelowna 1st ward. Following the call, we couldn't sleep as we told him we would be in Kelowna next Sunday and did not intend to miss this important calling. We are too wired to sleep so I get on the internet and start to find flights to Canada. At 1:00am we go to bed with an idea of the flight schedules. The next morning, after I had been to the travel agent and made tentative arrangements for the flight, Andrew called to say he will give us his air mile points if we can get to Puerto Vallarta and fly Alaska air. We fly into Kelowna Saturday morning after a night stopover in Seattle.

Sunday August 25/02.

We are sitting in church and when his name is called as Bishop of 1st ward and tears come to my eyes, for I knew this was a prayer answered. Andrew was ready for this calling. As I stood and placed my hands on his head - together with President Burnham, who set him apart - the spirit was so strong.

We spent the next week with the family and had a wonderful time. The next Sunday, September 1st. Andrew conducts his first sacrament meeting and he seemed very much in control.

Kelowna 1st. ward Bishopric.

2002. 8. 25 14:41

Sunday September 8 / 2002

Today we are sitting in Sidney ward sacrament service and Corey Holmes has just been sustained as a Deacon. Following the opening exercises of priesthood, Brian conferred the Aaronic priesthood and ordained him a deacon. I am able to be in the circle and feel of the spirit. This was an extra bonus for being in Victoria. Corey had wanted us to be here but as we had only been in Victoria last May we knew this was going to be impossible.

Heavenly Father moves in a wonderful way.

We had arrived in Victoria on September 3/02 and kept it a surprise from the grandchildren. You should have seen their faces. They knew who we were, but we were not supposed to be there.

While with Tanya and Brian, we have been looking at houses, units with a granny suite for us. Jenny and I need a base and also a place to store our furniture.

Sitting in church I felt out of place. It is surprising how only after 12 months in Mexico and working with the members in Ajijic ward we feel disassociated from Victoria. Not our friends, just the church. How can I say it? The church in Victoria is so formal. Everything is regimental. In Ajijic the spirit is always there but the feeling is more relaxed.

We leave on September 11/02, and our friends Mike and Jane will meet us in PA. Then after two days at the beach, we drove back to Ajijic.

Septiebre 16 I 2002

Yesterday was Independence Day but as it was a Sunday this year the Stake Centre in Guadalajara. had a big fiesta on Saturday evening. It started at 5pm with different wards bringing the traditional foods. I cannot seem to adapt to the taste of Tamales and after hearing of how they make them with tons of lard maybe it's just as well. There were tostadas, which is a crispy tortilla topped with beef or chicken, beans and a great sauce, they were good. Lots of other different foods which I have no idea what it was. I didn't try them.

Following the food there was dancing; the gym floor is full of people dancing all the time. There were children, babies, parents, grandparents of all ages bogeying away - they knew the movements.

The dancing stopped at 10pm, when the Mariachi Band arrived with much fanfare. The audience makes this incredible noise, a cross between a yodel and a scream. It is very much a Mexican sound, this is done at certain intervals. Everyone sings along. It is such fun.

At 11pm they shout, " Viva Mexico" then they continue to" Viva" all those who had a part in the revolution and ring bells, as this is how the people were called to revolt against the Spaniards. It is incredible seeing these humble people so full of patriotism towards their country, we could certainly learn from them.

Septiembre 22 / 2002

We just got home from the birthday party for Fransico's De Anda's baby. This has been one of the highlights of our stay here. We were treated like honoured guests. They live at the end of a street in San Nicholas. When we arrived at the party, they had borrowed a marquee that covered the street from one side to the other. Tables and chairs were set up in the street; there was an outside kiosk that the cooking was done on. So many smiles from everyone, the children find us a curiosity. It was wonderful. Jenny got to hold this 8-month-old baby the whole time as she fell asleep on her lap; she is so chubby and absolutely gorgeous!

We were served this stew (?) and crispy tortillas, followed by two tamales; I was too full to eat them. Gradually children seemed to come from everywhere until there were between 25- 30 kids. The children are so incredibly good looking. Next, the piñata was strung up across the street, first the big kids had their turn and when it broke open, they strung up another for the little ones. The 1yr old birthday boy got the first swing while in his mother's arms (he can't walk yet) and next they brought out this huge cake and a jelly type mixture - it was all delicious.

All the time there was music playing, and the kids were dancing and playing, it truly was an incredible afternoon. Anyway, we were so grateful to Fransico for inviting us. We are home now and too stuffed to move!

Octubre 6 | 2002

Oh, what a wonderful general conference from Salt Lake. Jenny and I watched Saturday and Sunday afternoon on the Internet. I drove the members to the stake centre in Guadalajara for the Sunday morning session and also priesthood Saturday night.

The stake has been able to set up the receiver so that we can have it in English as well as Spanish. Which makes it so much better.

We are so thankful for the Internet. With the church not as strong as at home we need the entire spiritual uplift we can get. The faithful members are strong, and we love their spirit, but the numbers are few.

Octubre 10 | 2002

Yes, I do have fun. With the school project finished I looked around for another volunteer program, not realizing that the bishop may be out of the county for two or more months.

I came across an article about Joe. Joe, a 70yr old man started a carpentry school for the nino's 4 years ago, and with the help of the local community managed to equip a classroom with carpentry equipment. Joe and his wife decided that this was a worthwhile project so have done without a gardener and maid, and with savings, spent it on buying wood for the school. The classroom is part of a building housing the social services in San Antonio. Every Martes and Jueves tardes from 3-5pm, I have volunteered to assist with a carpentry instruction. The nino's select ideas from books which are all in English and we make a list of the material required. The nino's find the wood at the back of the classroom, cut it to size and assemble. Some of the older nino's make quite elaborate items. Joe himself makes furniture on the off days, and sells them, using the money to buy either wood or new equipment.

Octubre 15 / 2002

Jenny's Thoughts

We have really struggled down here for the last couple of months. We love Mexico. I don't see how anyone cannot, never-the-less the Church is a big challenge. This is something new for us. We have always been surrounded by strong wards with good leadership. It can be difficult. .

It would appear Ajijic has suffered through a unique set of circumstances in the last few years. I think we might have headed back sooner but the Stake Pres. has said we are really needed here, so for now, we will stay. Derek is totally on his own. The Bishop is in the States for medical treatment, has been gone for three weeks with many more to go. The 2nd counselor is also in the States on business for the next three weeks. Both missionaries are Mexican, one with a little English, so we have no translators. Derek has written out all his introductions in Spanish, so he reads them. There is only one other Americano I can talk to and she leaves in two weeks! We feel a real bond with the members even though we can only converse in a small way. I do not write this to sound discouraged, only to say that it is not just one big holiday. We have made some good English-speaking friends outside of the church that we get to do things with.

Yesterday, was the Purepecha Festival. The festival is a wonderful mix of symbols from prehepatic and Christian eras. The Purepecha empire, known as the Tarascans to the Spanish Conquistadors, flourished in the state of Michoacan from about 1100 AD to 1530 AD. They brought their customs and crafts to Ajijic, the street decorations were spectacular, and their dancing wonderful. The amount of clothes the children wore was amazing; it was a hot, hot day. They have at least 4 skirts on (and long pants under that) thick flannel shirts x 2, scarves around their neck and lower face as well as their heads. All of this is decorated with flowers or glitter of some kind. Then they dance in the hot sun, a very lively dance.

Even though Derek's head was covered in sunscreen, he got burnt. We bought him a Mexican straw hat! They had all their crafts for sale - things like shoes, dresses, hats, straw work, pottery, food etc. I think what makes everything so celebratory down here is that it always includes the whole family. The street designs are all made of flowers.

Octubre 29 | 2002

Today I am 60 years old. I feel no difference, should I? At this point in my life, I am thankful for being in Mexico. As I sat in the garden today, with the sun shining, I stretched out my hand and a butterfly landed on my hand, just 12 inches from my face. I looked into its eyes, thinking "what do you see?" I lifted it from my hand and let it fly away.

Earlier in the day I went to my carpentry class. The boys were a little hyper, but we all had a good time. It's strange, these boys always seem to be in a rush to complete their projects, and yet the Mexican way is to go slow.

Jenny and I have agreed not to go out and celebrate our respective birthdays; rather we will spend the money on enjoying our grandchildren when they arrive Noviebre 4/02.

Although we are enjoying Ajijic, I still miss the ocean. So, I feel that when the time comes for us to find a winter retreat, I would think I will look towards the coast.

Grandma is such a strength to me. I love her very much. She helps me view the right perspective of the various situations I find myself in. We had a long talk last Sunday and came to the conclusion that the only way we are going to help the church in Ajijic is to let the members become responsible for it. We are not going to pay for items required. The wards are going to. We are not always going to be here, and it means that those who follow have a harder time continuing with the ward. Members are to make their own way to church unless a member is going past their casa. For those poor we will give some bus money to them, but not on a regular basis. Some members are truly converted, others just lukewarm.

If we only have 20 members to sacrament so be it. Those 20 will grow in faith and love of the gospel. I hope Heavenly Father understands our reasoning. We will continue to visit all the members to encourage them to come to church.

Noviembre 19 / 2002

Well, Tanya and family have been here for two weeks. We spent the first week in Puerto Vallarta in a wonderful house overlooking the bay at Sayulita.

During this time, we experienced watching dolphins at play in the bay, visited the damage done by Hurricane Kenna, and played with the grandchildren in the high surf. The sun shone most of the time.

Since coming to Ajijic the children have attended church and were not able to understand a word of the sacrament due to it all being in Spanish. Tanya did take the young ones into primary and gave a lesson in English. Corey came to priesthood and we translated it for him.

Tanya homeschools in the mornings, and I take the boys twice a week to a carpentry class for two hours. They must make items that can be transported on the plane. On Wednesday they go with Tanya to beginners Spanish lessons for one and a half hours.

Today they visited Oak Hill School, a bi-lingual school in Ajijic. The principal has agreed to let them, that is Corey, Jeffrey and Emma, attend school for the remaining time before Christmas. Corey is a little apprehensive, but each of the grandchildren knows one child their age because they are members of the church. These same children have started to come and play at our house following school.

Last Friday, Emma and Savannah came to the handicap horse-riding program. Following the program, we gave each of them a ride on the horses. Savannah was thrilled.

Diciembre 9 / 2002

Since the middle of Noviembre the weather has been below seasonal average. Each morning we have had to light the gas heater to take the chill of the house. The days have warmed up to 25 degs.

Yesterday, Diciembre 8/02, the primary presentation was the sacrament meeting. Tanya had been asked by Laura McCombs to assist, so Tanya involved the children. It was wonderful. The children each had a part in the presentation, and Elder Zimmerman translated the talk. Savannah was very cute sitting on her seat, not understanding a word that was being said. Corey was nervous but the talk was on temples, that being the theme for this year

During the last two weeks here, we have tried to involve the family in the church activities. The language is a barrier, but they seem to overcome the problem.

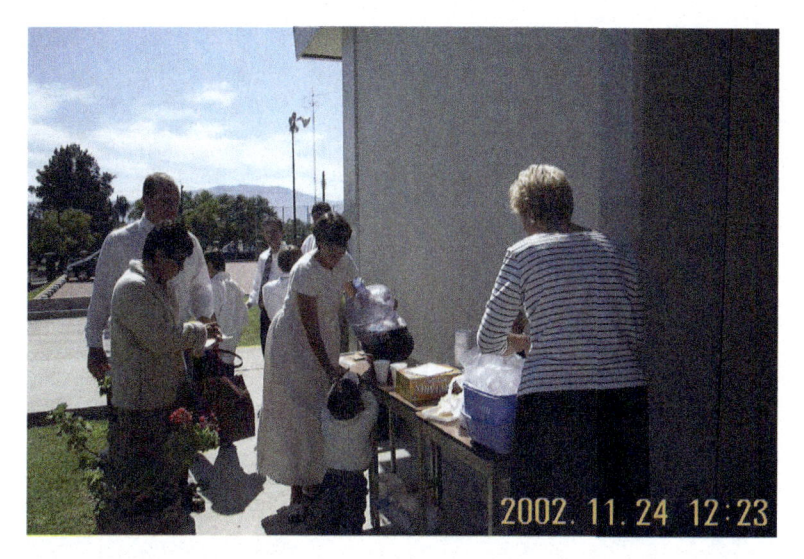

During church time yesterday I spoke to the Estaca President regarding our remaining time in Ajijic. I informed him that we are planning to return to Canada in March, feeling that we had served a mission by helping the ward for the last 18 months. He asked if we would be returning later, to which I replied that we had not made any decisions at this point. Jenny and I feel we need to return to Canada so that we can strengthen our relationship and testimonies. The language has been a barrier between the members and us. Although we are able to talk to them it has been on a limited basis. It may be that when we go on an official mission for the church, it will be an English-speaking mission. We leave it in the Lord's hands.

Diciembre 14 / 2002

We are sitting on the beach at Sayulita for a week of relaxation. Brian arrived on Dic. 10 and has taken over entertaining the grandchildren.

On our way out we stopped at Ixtlan del Rio, which has ancient ruins. Jeffrey said he wants to be an archeologist when he grows up. The rock formations were very interesting, each depicting either a house, altar or sports area.

Ixtlan del Rio 2002. 12. 14 12:38

The weather at the coast is wonderful. I mentioned to Emma that this is like the garden of Eden, her reply " If this is like the Garden of Eden, where are the apple trees" Wonderful thought.

As always the grandchildren had fun, except the waves in the ocean were too high due to a storm condition in California.

Diciembre 19 l2002

You never know when you will be called upon to use your priesthood. Today when we went to pick up some of Tanya's luggage, (this luggage had been taken out to the village by some friends) in Los Marco, a village north of Sayulita, the woman asked if I was a member of the LDS church. Telling her that I was, and that she was also, she asked if I would give a blessing to her mother. Her mother was not a member but had faith that we could help her. Brian, my son-in-law was with me, so gave me assistance. Not knowing the outcome, one can only pray that she accepted the blessing and she gained strength from it.

Diciembre 24 l 2002

We have just returned from giving out Christmas stockings that Tanya had made and the children had filled with candies and small toys.

We drove into San Juan Cosala, a village 20 minutes from Ajijic, and stopped just outside the village plaza. Corey and Emma went to give stockings to two small children. When the rest of the children saw what was happening, they all started to run to the van. We must have had 20-30 children around the car.

Unfortunately Tanya had made only 43 stockings so some children went away empty handed. The grandchildren were so excited at seeing all the children. The experience was wonderful for them. It put them in the Christmas spirit.

Tonight we are going to a pasada in San Antonio. This is where they reenact the Christmas story.

I think then the children will be ready for Christmas.

Enero 7 I 2003

    We have just returned from taking Tanya and family, together with the dogs (yes, both), to Puerto Vallarta for their return trip to Canada. Tanya and the children agreed to take the dogs, as it would be easier for us to travel for the next three months. The two months have gone so fast, but I think we packed a great deal of excitement into it.

One van-16 bags-8 persons-2 dogs off to airport.
2003. 1. 6 10:55

    The last two weeks have been the most exciting, with Christmas being the main joy. As always the children seemed to get more presents than ever.

    During this time we went horse riding, visited the health spa at San Juan Cosala, celebrated Jeffrey's birthday, and hiked up the mountain behind us. The hike, which took three hours, was a little much for the girls but they managed it.

Last Sunday, Dec 29, Mike Hainsworth invited us all over for a BBQ, which was great because he had a large garden so the children were able to run and play.

Now Jenny and I have to continue with our plans. We have given our notice to the owners of the house, and will be leaving Mexico on Feb 2 2003. We are going to England, leaving our van with all our possessions in San Antonio, Texas for the month. Jenny is not so well, so rather than wait until we get to Victoria we decided to go now. Upon our return to Texas, we will just meander back to Victoria, probably arriving mid April.

My Thoughts On Mexico

It has been a wonderful experience. We have met so many wonderful people, both Mexican and North Americans. The church has been disappointing, but this is due in part to me not being able to learn the language sufficiently to communicate with them. Someday, who knows, I may be able to master it, but for the time being I must resign myself to the fact that languages aren't my strong point. We never know what impact we have on a community or the church until you leave. I hope that at least someone's life has been changed for the better by our being here. Time will tell. The main thing is we have been blessed with good health, and safety while driving. It was our one concern when we left Canada.

January 12 / 2003

Today I was released as 1st. counselor in the Ajijic bishopric. Jenny was also released as the Young Women's president. Although we had to be released, it is with some sadness, as many members expressed their thanks for our time here and asked when we will return. With uncertainty in our lives we are not able to answer that question. The next two weeks before leaving for England we'll take it easy. We are spending our Tuesday's out at the spa at San Juan Cosala. The water is from a natural spring and it services three pools, all at different temperatures. It also has a steam room area underground and a jetted tub at ground level. We take lunch with us and make a day of it.

January23 / 2003

Last night at 8.15pm we had an earthquake.

The centre of the quake was in Colima about 3 hours west from Ajijic, on the pacific coast. Our house started to roll and sway. I felt like I was on a boat in the ocean. It lasted only minutes but seemed longer. From reports, it was 7.8 on the Richter scale and caused much damage in Colima. About 23 lost their lives. In Guadalajara, 40 houses collapsed, but in Ajijic most damage was the cracking of walls.

January 26 | 2003

    Today we went into Guadalajara to Degollado Teatro to see the University of Guadalajara Ballet Folclórico.

    We last saw them in Feb. 2001 and this show was still just as fabulous. They have been in existence for 35 years, and have performed in front of hundreds and hundreds of people on Sunday mornings. They have performed tours in more than 20 countries (and on every continent). They received recognitions, representing Mexico culture, as countless young students learn to love traditions by dancing them. Generations of university students and teachers have passed on the gift of their knowledge to younger dancers, which has meant that important cultural dances have been conserved and traditions which otherwise would have been lost in the region of origin. Although the ballet specializes in regional traditions, something is created on stage, which goes beyond the 'folkloric.' It's something very primitive. It is the body in motion, so we are charmed by the turns and leaps of the dancers. They give pleasure, joy and delight to us the audience.

January 27 | 2003

    This was Jenny's day. Jenny has become involved with an orphanage called Villa Infantil de Nuestra Sra. Located on the south shore of the lake, the orphanage just opened in 2002 and at present has 18 children. It is run by three nuns but has no support from the Catholic Church. The children are housed in two casas, with one nun overseeing each casa.

The reason for Jenny to go (and for me to tag along) was to celebrate the birthday of two of the children. One lady from when the orphanage was first opened was providing the food from her own resources. There is no funding in place. Today they still rely on donations from the community.

Jenny brought them all the food that we have no use for - as we're leaving soon - and the clothes that Tanya left behind at Christmas. The Americans and Canadians that came to the party have so much love for the children. One couple, Dave and Darleen Pike, spend many days going to the orphanage to either play with the children or to repair toys and generally assist where needed.

February 5 I 2003

The time is 13:41, Wednesday Feb. 5, and Jenny and I are on the plane on our way to England. Time seems to be flying. Excuse the pun! We left Mexico on February 2nd 2003 with much uncertainty as to whether we will return. Jane and Mick, our very good friends, will be missed by us, and we them.

We had a wonderful ride from Ajijic to Nuevo Laredo on the Mexican-US. border. The weather was clear and warm all the way. By taking the toll roads, through San Lois Potosi and onto Monterrey and then Nuevo Laredo, the 11 hours seemed to pass by quickly. The van was completely full to the roof and above.

We spent Monday in Laredo, Texas arranging car insurance and Tuesday and Wednesday morning were spent in San Antonio Texas. Jenny had a marvellous time going shopping. The malls filled her with wonderment as to the assortment of clothes. We are both trying to be good at not overspending.

We will be in London until March 5th 2003 visiting with my mother.

Chapter 26 | Thoughts On England

It is Valentines Day, and we have been in England for just over a week.

What has happened? Well, one big thing is that my mum is looking well and healthy, which was a great relief to us both. I feel she is pleased to see us.

On Feb 12th it was my mother's 85th birthday. I took mum and Auntie Betty to the salvation army church for their sunshine club meeting. They sung Happy Birthday to her and the meeting was centred around Valentines Day. Mum enjoyed all the attention. In the evening, 24 family and friends came to a party at Denis and Steven's home (my brother) and wished her a Happy Birthday.

Yesterday was a great day. Barry and Pauline Stewart (our friends from Victoria), stopped in London on their way back to Victoria from Dubai. We arranged to meet in their hotel at 10:00am and in doing so, were able to catch up on the entire going-ons in Victoria.

We had a wonderful day. We had lunch prior to going to the theatre in the afternoon and seeing 'No Stones In My Shoes.' Following the show we had a snack as we then decided to take in the musical "Chicago"

February 15l 2003

We are now in Breadwardine and will spend the week with Eileen, Jenny's sister. Our first surprise was waking up to snow on Monday morning. It was only a sprinkle and gone by lunchtime. I've walked around the hillsides each morning and it was wonderful to smell the fresh air. We feel we could stay here during the summer, but not the winter.

I think the highlight for Jenny was having her Uncle Jack Smith talk about his life, which of course was also relating to Jenny's mum, as he is her half brother.

While in Hereford we went to the market, and as it was cold we purchased some more warm sweaters. We went to *Trafalgar Square*, then up to Oxford Street. Jenny had to look at the shops. The prices scared her off though. We finished the evening off by going to the theatre and seeing 'Phantom of the Opera. '

Chapter 27 | Across The Ocean

March 6 | 2003

    We arrived in San Antonio last night at 8:30pm. The return flight from England seemed to take forever. Probably due to the fact that we had to go into Chicago and wait 3.5 hours before our flight to San Antonio. Chicago had 5 inches of snow the night before, but was only snowing lightly when we landed. It did not delay us.

    It was hard saying goodbye to my mum, knowing that we may not see her again. I have promised the family that we will return next year. Mum seemed to be in good spirits when we left, but that may have been due to the fact that we had been there to keep her company.

    I suppose if our money had been able to go further, we may have considered renting a flat and staying longer but this was only a dream.

    We just have to pray that mum will continue to stay healthy.

    Today we spent the day visiting the Alamo and the river walk area of San Antonio. The Alamo history is unknown to us other than David Crockett. The river walk area is a beautiful walk, following the river through the downtown area. On each side of the river are restaurants on the sidewalk and ferry boats taking people on guided tours through the river maze. The river is only 30 feet across and is kept in beautiful condition.

March 11 / 2003

    We have been in Scottsdale AZ. now for three days, and the weather is beautiful. We plan to spend at least two weeks here, possibly three, depending on the weather up north in Canada. After being cold in England, we cannot face any cold weather for awhile. We feel that this is a rest stop, and holiday, as we have no commitments or obligations to anyone. Our time is our own, just to laze in the pool, and do laps the sun. The plan is still to arrive in Victoria for the first week of April.

March 21 / 2003

    We are preparing to leave Scottsdale, AZ tomorrow heading up to Las Vegas and arriving in Victoria around March 29. The time spent here has been wonderful. We spent last Tuesday afternoon at the Mesa temple. We needed to get a feeling of where our life was going. Both Jenny and I feel that we should stop worrying at this point. The Lord has made it known that all will be well, and that we only need to be thankful for what we have. We will make plans for the near future, and see what crosses our path.

    While here, we have also visited various retirement communities. The facilities are nice, but feel this is not for us at this time. You could only spend the winters here. The summers would be too hot.

    We did visit the botanical gardens, and although pleasant to walk around, it comes nowhere near the beauty of Buchart Gardens in Victoria. Whenever we mention to people where we are from, it is surprising the amount of people that have visited Victoria. We probably take it for granted.

I should mention that we went to church on Sunday, and were overwhelmed by the amount in attendance. It takes some getting used to going from the 40 members in Ajijic to the 200 in Scottsdale.

March 22 | 2003

On the road again. We're driving from Scottsdale heading to Bakersfield, California. What a different drive than it was 19 months ago. The hills and valleys are green and beautiful to view, from San Bernido up to Bakersville.

Travelling through the Palms Springs and Desert Springs area, one cannot help to notice all the wind generating power units.

March 24 | 2003

Today we arrived in Crescent City, California. We left Sacramento this morning at 10: 30, having spent 2 hours walking around Sacramento's old town.

John Sutter settled the area in 1845 at about the same time of the California gold rush, and the town is trying to restore to its original state. On the waterfront dock there is an old paddle steamer, which has been converted to a hotel. As the railway system operated from the waterfront on the Southern Pacific, they have laid out the trains and carriages as a museum.

The buildings for three blocks have been restored and the sidewalks have been raised, and constructed of wood. The roads are cobble - as per the period.

March 27 | 2003

The time is 4:00pm and we are sitting in our motel in Port Angeles. The weather has not been nice the last 3 days. We had hoped to spend some time walking on the beach in Oregon, but the rain was on and off most of the time. We did walk for about 30 minutes just before Lincoln City.

Chapter 28 | Home Again

As we get ready to take the ferry home tomorrow, we are apprehensive about what the next months hold for us.

Looking back over the last 19 months - and having been out of Mexico for almost two months - our feelings of what we have left behind are mixed. On the one hand it will be good to see the family, but on the other hand the experience of living in Mexico was priceless. The next six months will tell.

Whatever the outcome we have been blessed with safety and good health.

Stepping back onto Canadian soil in March 2003 we had no idea how the next few years would unfold. Firstly, not knowing where our life is going yet, we have decided to rent a condo on the 16th floor of Toronto Street in Victoria. From the 16th floor we have a view of the ocean. Being afraid of heights I felt a little trepidation going onto the balcony.

Going to church in Victoria 1st ward was a new experience for us - as for the last 19 months we have only heard messages in Spanish. Being able to hear the gospel in English gave me a great spiritual uplift and not knowing many members in the ward felt like we were starting all over again.

Up until this time our homes have always been in 2nd ward, so except for some members in 1st ward that we knew though activities, we had to start getting to know everyone.

1st ward is an inner city ward, covering an area from Oak Bay to the downtown area with a diverse social membership.

It was on one Sunday in May 2003 that the Stake President (Randy Keys) asked to speak with me. I had no inkling that I would be called as the bishop because I had found out previously that the present bishop had only be called 2 years earlier. When he said that he would like to extend the calling of bishop for 1st. ward, I had to ask him to repeat it, as it was not what I had expected to hear him say.

He then said for me to discuss it with Sister Draper....Jenny. I should mention that up until this point, since returning from Mexico, we had thought about going to Australia for year or two.

Well...this now changed our thinking.

Chapter 29 | Service To Others

It was on August 17th 2003 when I was sustained a Bishop of the Victoria 1st ward, and our whole life took a different path.

Firstly we knew we were going to be in 1st ward for 5 years so we set about finding a home within the ward boundaries. Secondly, it became a high priority for me to get to know the members - and they also get to know me. I realized from the time of being called, most had not even heard my name or did not know me yet.

Although I will not dwell on my time as Bishop, I would like to mention a few of my spiritual and fondest memories of this time.

The first one was the deep love I had for each member, some coming from humble beginnings and seeing their willingness to serve.

I also had an open door for anyone who wanted to come and talk about anything of concern to them.

Second, the primary children.

With permission from the parents I became the candy Bishop, as following services each Sunday the door was open for the primary children (and even the youth) to come by, talk, and take a candy.

As I was not working since coming back from Mexico, all my appointments regarding church related matters were during the week. This allowed me to have my door (and schedule) open on Sunday.

Within a few months of being sustained as Bishop, it was required of me to perform my first of many funerals. These totalled to 15 by the time I was released. I had not been to many funerals, let alone performed the service. With my Father in Heavens help all went well, and the member was laid to rest in the ground with a happy send off.

Chapter 30 | Renovating Desire Returns

Realizing that we needed to have a place of our own, we set about in 2004 looking for a house to purchase. Our criteria was that it would be in need of renovations, so we found a townhouse on Swan Street, which as you probably guessed, met our requirements.

So after installing new windows and reconfiguring the bathroom - which took about two months, and happened prior to moving in - we packed up our boxes and furniture in Toronto Street, and moved into Swan Street.

What was interesting regarding this renovation was outside Toronto Street was a bus stop with a bus that went directly to Swan Street. This meant Jenny could have the use of the car and come along later with meals on wheels to keep me energized for the day. This also allowed me to be able to leave early in the morning before Jenny had even stirred.

Well, the renovation bug had hit, so off we went to look for another project which came in the form of a small house on Lodge Street. This was just around the corner from Swan Street and it was small (just under a 1000 sq. ft), but it fit our needs.

Because of some problems with occupancy (it having been a rental property with tenants needing two months notice to vacate), we were not able to start the interior demolition work, so we took off. We left my 1st counsellor to guide the affairs of Victoria 1st ward - all with the Stake Presidents approval.

The renovation turned out to be a total refit, from removing the fireplace chimney brick by brick to installing a 16ft bearing beam which allowed us to open up the living room to the kitchen / eating area. Then the kitchen got a redesign - including part of the ceiling, which was falling down during the wall removal - and finally a new ensuite bathroom.

Oh the joys of renovations! Or not joyful - depends how you look at it

As you must by now have realized, we did not live in the house for those two months because we had the use of a friends condo while they were away for the winter.

Chapter 31 | Refilling the Retirement Vessel

Feeling I needed to do some form of work, other that taking care of the Victoria 1st wards needs. So in 2006 I applied for a position with Habitat for Humanity which would involve managing / supervising the construction of low income homes. The work was done by volunteer's together with professional trades people when the need arose. The background of Habitat for Humanity is a non-profit, providing homes for families unable to qualify for conventional mortgages. This would provide them with a home at a cost they would be able to pay - and family stability for 25 years. Another part of the family's requirement was that they would also volunteer 500 hours of their time - whether it be doing the actual construction or service in the habitat stores. The actual construction was a challenge, as during the week only a few volunteers could come to the worksite. In most cases, they were former trades people so required no training, only direction, as to what was needed to be done. The biggest challenge came on Saturdays when up to 20 persons would turn up (both male and female), each with a hammer ready to drive nails into wood.

After the first 3 months I realized that the progress made each week and the timeframe given to complete each house did not match up. Building at this rate it would take years. In fact, the previous houses had taken over 3 years.

I approached management with the idea of asking Camosun College in Victoria if they would like to use our houses as a training program for their construction course. For the next two projects, the basic framing to lock up was completed by Camosun College students, with the work being performed 3 days a week and the volunteers still coming on Saturdays.

I also approached various electrical and plumbing contractors asking if they would like to volunteer their workers to rough in their work, with one contractor volunteering to do the complete rough-in and completion of the plumbing.

Chapter 32 | Step Back To Travel

What would my life story be without mention of our travels?

Traveling has been one of our great times; being able to visit many parts of the world, whether cruising or flying to various destinations and getting to know the local people.

We have been blessed to have seen most of the world and grown to appreciate the wonderful country of Canada we live in and call home. Looking back at some of the counties we have visited, our trip to the Holy Land is the most memorable.

We stood in the amphitheatre where Paul spoke to the Ephesians,

and went to the river Jordon, where John The Baptist baptized Jesus.

Sea of Galilee

We also went to the Mount Of Olives, where Jesus preached looking down from the mount onto the Garden of Gethesmane in the background.

We were able to walk through Jerusalem (where Jesus also walked), and Capernaum and Nazareth as well.

Custodia Terrae Sanctae
CAPHARNAUM
Capharnaum the town of Jesus
The House of Simon Peter
The Synagogue

Wailing Wall in Jerusalem

In Bethlehem, where Jesus was born.

The Dead Sea

BYU Jerusalem

We also visited the Mayan ruins in Mexico and ancient castles in England.

Then there was the time we spent Christmas in Antigua, when Jason, Tanya, Brian, Andrew Shelley and the young ones (Alex, Zak and Corey), came to be with us on our extended stay in the Caribbean.

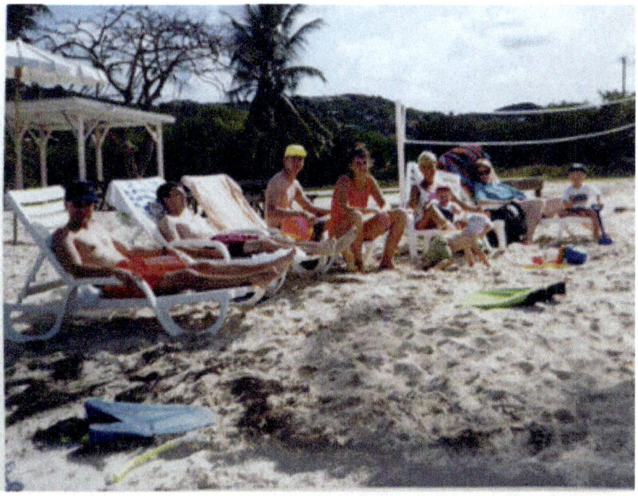

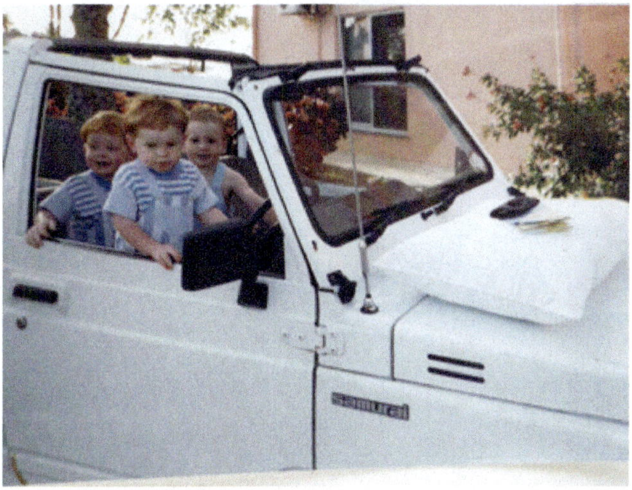

While there we witnessed the birth of baby tortoise!

Chapter 33 | Moving Forward

Now I come to the time to which some of my grandchildren can relate to and remember.

In 2008 the Holmes family and ourselves purchased a 1 1/4 acre country property, coming with a home, together with a cottage which we lived in. It was in North Saanich, on Vancouver Island.

I felt it was a great experience for the grandchildren, as during that time they had chickens to raise and collect eggs, three pigs fattened up by Jeff for the market, goats to provide milk, and giving birth to little ones, Savannah's miniature horse (whose only desire was to get loose), and raccoons who felt that the chickens were for their meals. And of course turkeys for the festive seasons.

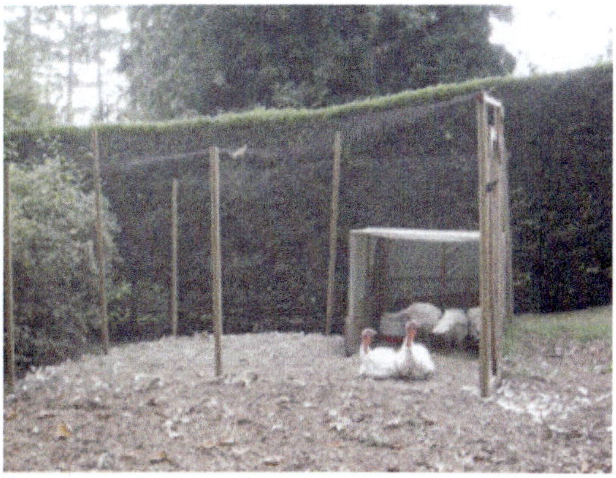

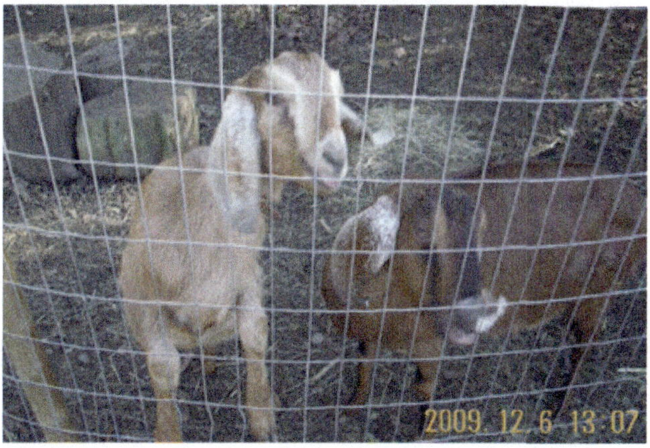
2009. 12. 6 13:07

A treehouse was constructed with a ladder to reach the room at the top, and a play house to study in or for a bit of peace and quiet.

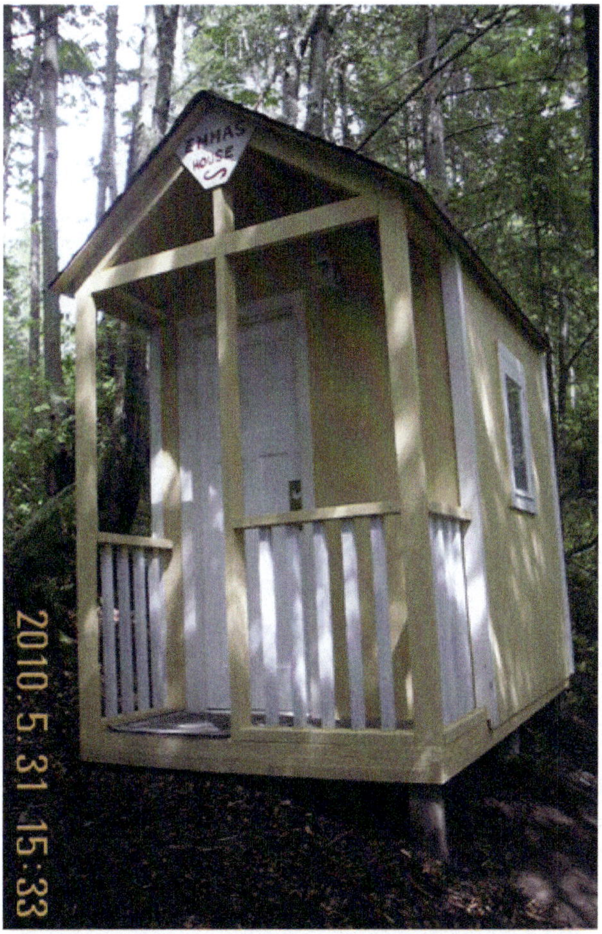
EMMAS
HOUSE
2010 5 31 15:33

Because music was a big part of the Holmes life, a music room was built. I should say, it was actually converted from a single carport. Thirty feet from the main house made it just outside of being heard when full drums, piano and any other instrument were being played.

The year of 2013 was our 50th wedding anniversary so the weekend of October 8th some of the family joined us to celebrate it at the Pink Palace, in White Rock BC. That was not its real name but it was pink in colour.

Accommodation at the hotel was from Friday night until Sunday lunch time, with Saturday morning watching General Conference from Salt Lake and the afternoon being spent at the beach in White Rock.

Saturday evening we all met for a banquet meal and music entertainment provided by the grandchildren, with Sunday morning listen to General Conference followed by a buffet lunch at the hotel. It was wonderful to see all the children enjoying themselves.

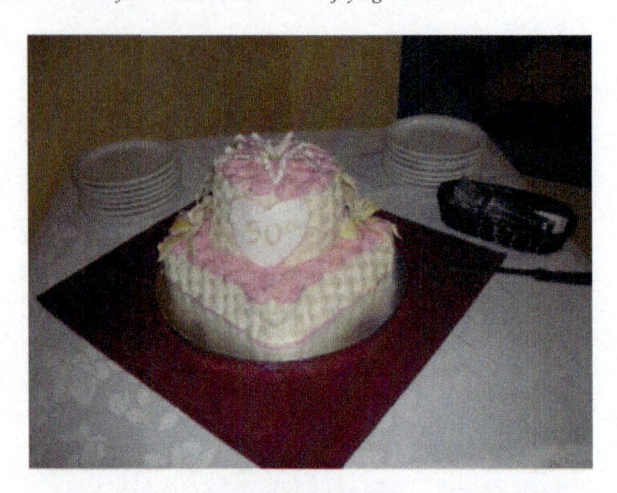

Our anniversary cake

Zak and Alex playing music

Watching conference in the hotel room

Photo of the family, missing Jason and family, as well as Jeffrey who was serving his mission.

As in life all good things must come to an end, so in 2014 Tanya, Brian and their children departed for Uganda to start another path of life. Jenny and I moved into the main house on Tatlow, to which some of the older grandchildren came and stayed with us while going to college.

I would amiss if I did not give thanks to my wonderful wife, mother, grandmother, great grandmother (Gi Gi) and the devotion she has for children.

Chapter 34 | Present Day

Jumping forward to present day where we have three children.

Andrew, who with Shelley has three children, Alex, Zak and Rachel.

Tanya, who with Brian has nine children, Corey, Jeffrey, Emma, Savannah, Liam, Treymaine, Christian, Jesse and Mia.

Jason, who with Michelle has eight children, Ammon, Caleb, Jonah, Lucas, Timandra, Rebekah, Gideon, and Sirena.

This makes for 20 grandchildren.

Zak & Andrea started the great grandchildren line by having Emryn.

Jeffrey & Ali came along with Lucy and Jack.

Rachel & Braden have Eleanor and Maverick.

Alex & Sarah have Lark, with one also due in December 2023

Emma & Rodolfo have Sammie & Lillie.

This brings the total great grandchildren to eight with more on the way.

What would our life have been like if firstly we had not come to Canada in 1965, if I had not accepted to work in Lethbridge in 1971?

I feel it was Heavenly Fathers plan for us.

It is interesting having been born in England that our son, Andrew served his mission in the London Bristol mission, our granddaughter, Emma in the Manchester mission, and our other granddaughter, Savannah called to the Scotland Ireland mission but was not able to go because of the COVID-19 virus of 2020.

God moves in mysterious ways. His wonders to perform.

I had never heard of the church of Jesus Christ of Latter-Day Saints, and never came across a missionary in England or Canada before 1971

Both jenny and I have served in many callings and have grown closer to our Father in Heaven over the years.

I pray that as you read this book, which I dedicate to my posterity, it will give you an insight into my life's journey, realizing that our Heavenly Fathers plan is for us all to be with Him someday.

For me it will be sooner than those that read this book,

In the end, hopefully, we will all be reunited together in Heaven.

Chapter 35 | Thoughts About Life

"Let no one ever come to you without leaving better and happier."

"If you do not like the road you are walking, start paving another one"

*"Do not wait until the conditions are perfect to begin.
Beginning makes the conditions perfect"*

"What lies behind you and what lies in front of you, pales in comparison to what lies inside of you"

I would be amiss if I did not finish this story of my life (so far), without my testimony of the truthfulness of the gospel of Jesus Christ. It has been a special part of my life and through the guidance of the Holy Ghost, it became part of my life and Jenny's since 1972. I know that God lives and Jesus Christ is my Saviour and in the not to distance future I will come before him and hopefully be welcomed into His kingdom. May His light continually rest upon each of you also throughout your lives. This is my prayer.

My love to all of you.

Husband. Father. Grandpa. Papa.
Derek Draper.
2023
The year of our 60th wedding anniversary (and my 81st birthday year)